DIY Financial Planning
how to get the life you want

by

Jane Wheeler
BSc (Sp Hons) FIFP CFP^{CM} APFS

D1256596

Fourth Edition

Published 2011 by arima publishing

www.arimapublishing.com

ISBN 978 1 84549 527 5

© Jane Wheeler 2011

First edition published 2008

Revised printing 2009, 2010, 2011

Printed and bound in the United Kingdom

Typeset in Palatino Linotype & Arial

arima publishing

ASK House, Northgate Avenue

Bury St Edmunds, Suffolk IP32 6BB

t: (+44) 01284 700321

www.arimapublishing.com

Message from the author

I hope this book will be a real help to you in trying to get your financial life on track. It is intended to be short and easy to read and to help you to realise what is really important to you and then to achieve it.

I have thought long and hard about whether the book should be available as an ebook and have come to the conclusion that, although we are living in the digital age, it would be more helpful to have a book that you can hold, have by the bed, on the kitchen worktop or on your desk – something that you can touch and keep coming back to: a 'friend' and support along the way.

To provide further support, we have set up a website for SORTED! readers at www.sortedfinancially.co.uk where you will be able to find up to date facts and figures as well as other items of interest and directions to other helpful websites. There is a free downloadable guide to the current tax details and details of legislation that you need to know about as well as a lot of other information which, hopefully, you will find of interest.

Good luck! If you stick at it you will get SORTED!

I am grateful to all those people who have encouraged me in the writing of this book and its earlier editions. In particular I should like to thank my husband David for his patience and support and Joceline Bury for her help in editing the book.

Jane Wheeler

Contents

Introduction

This short book will help you to get SORTED!, financially. You will learn to identify your real goals and objectives and how to achieve them through a process of financial planning.

If you are prepared to take responsibility, to put in the effort that is required at the beginning of this process and then to stick to your plan, then you will definitely be pleased that you embarked on this journey and you should read on. However - it is essential that you be honest with yourself (and your partner) here - if you are expecting someone else to do all the work for you, forget it now: you are not ready!

It's a very difficult time for many of us: the consequences of the recession have left many feeling helpless. It's up to us to change things for ourselves and this book aims to help you do it. Every situation represents an opportunity for the majority of us (rich, poor and in between) to reassess our priorities and to get ourselves 'SORTED!'.

In 1859, as the opening to his book 'A Tale of Two Cities', Charles Dickens wrote:

"It was the best of times, it was the worst of times; it was the age of wisdom, it was the age of foolishness: it was the epoch of belief, it was the epoch of incredulity; it was the season of Light, it was the season of Darkness; it was the spring of hope, it was the winter of despair; we had everything before us, we had nothing before us."

Go to the SORTED! website at www.sortedfinancially.co.uk for up to date information and to download your free guide to current tax data.

This could have been written about our own times.

The reality is that we are where we are and we need to find a way to improve our situation, ourselves. Remember, 'improve' does not mean buy more stuff, it means increase the things of real value in your life.

Unhappiness often comes from a lack of purpose, a sense that nothing you do makes any difference: that you are on the hamster wheel, life is passing by and you aren't really engaged. We can do something about this. If that's how you feel, let's try and change it! By focussing on what is important to us, we can be genuinely successful in achieving our goals.

Financial planning is still little understood in the UK. It's not about the sale or purchase of financial products, or about investment decisions, it's about realising what it is that we *really* want, being realistic and organising our financial affairs to be effective and to enable us to achieve our goals and dreams. It's generally an ongoing, progressive process and not a one-time fix.

One of the pioneers of financial planning in UK used to say:

"We never plan to fail, we just fail to plan."

Many people, perhaps like you, are looking for help in getting the impetus to put their financial house in order so that they can get to where they want to be.

Go to the SORTED! website at www.sortedfinancially.co.uk for up to date information and to download your free guide to current tax data.

2

Congratulations! By picking up this book, you have taken the first important step of acknowledging, to yourself at least, that you want to make changes and to improve your situation. The next step is to recognise that, if you want to change your situation, you will need to do things differently. As Einstein taught us, madness can be defined as doing the same thing over and over again and expecting different results.

Let's do things differently!

Getting Help

There is help available to us all and a lot of it is free. There are a lot of useful websites around – see the SORTED! website – and such organisations as The Money Advice Service, The Citizens Advice Bureau or the Institute of Financial Planning's *Financial Planning Week* can provide lots of information, tools and ideas helpful to everyone.

Look around, there is a lot of help out there if you spend time looking for it and it need not cost you a penny.

Professional help
If your affairs are complex and you feel you can afford to pay for professional help with this process then you should seek out an appropriately qualified financial planner. Visit the Institute of Financial Planning's website at www.financialplanning.org.uk and use the 'find a Certified Financial Planner' search for a professional in your area. Remember, financial products may not be what you need right

Go to the SORTED! website at www.sortedfinancially.co.uk for up to date information and to download your free guide to current tax data.

3

now. If you want to be sure that you find a firm that will give you genuine financial planning advice and not be interested only in persuading you to buy financial products then look on the same website for the register of 'Accredited Financial Planning Firms': with these firms you can be confident that you will receive a genuine planning service.

A professional planner can add a lot to the process but you need to bear in mind that this help will not be free.

DIY – doing it yourself

If the services of a financial planner are beyond you at the moment, or if your situation is straightforward enough to cope with yourself, then this book will help you to take control and sort things out for yourself. At the very least it will enable you to make a start on getting yourself and your life on track and provide you with a process to follow to get you there.

This book does NOT contain:

> ➢ Rocket science
> ➢ 'Hot' investment tips or in-depth investment advice
> ➢ Advanced tax planning advice

Go to the SORTED! website at www.sortedfinancially.co.uk for up to date information and to download your free guide to current tax data.

4

But it DOES contain:

> ➤ Encouragement to help you take control of your situation
> ➤ A framework for you to get on the right road to planning your future and realising your dreams.
> ➤ A reference point to come back to to refocus your energies, from time to time
> ➤ Some general observations about investment and what habits to try to avoid.

All your own work

Achieving your goals may not be easy - but then nothing that's worthwhile ever is! There is a process involved and it's important that you follow it step by step so you have a solid base on which to build. Don't try and find short cuts: you will only be fooling yourself.

Remember that anything you achieve will be your own work: allow yourself to take the credit.

Working with your partner, if you have one

For better or for worse, the process of financial planning will not be satisfactory if you and your partner are going in different directions. This whole process may pull you together and give you the great satisfaction of working on something together – but you should be prepared for it to trigger trouble if there is nothing you can agree as a joint goal or aspiration.

Go to the SORTED! website at www.sortedfinancially.co.uk for up to date information and to download your free guide to current tax data.

Everyone is different

Suggestions given in this book are necessarily generalised – you will need to decide if they work for you. Although your financial circumstances may be similar to many others, your objectives and your resources in terms of ambition and determination will be unique to you.

An ancient Chinese proverb teaches us:

"The person who moves a mountain begins by carrying away small stones."

Let's get started!

Go to the SORTED! website at www.sortedfinancially.co.uk for up to date information and to download your free guide to current tax data.

6

Where are you now?   1

Different priorities exist at different life stages but the same principles of financial planning apply and the same broad processes can be employed by everyone, whatever their age or situation. First, we need to understand how we really feel about things now and what we would like to change.

The Life Circle

This simple device, shown in Appendix 1, allows you to give a score of 1 – 5 (where 1 is really bad and 5 is excellent) to various aspects of your life. Take your time, work with your partner and take it seriously – record your answers in Appendix 1 and date it – there are three versions available so you can return to your Life Circle in the future and reassess your feelings about life.

You'll need to come back to your completed Life Circle later when considering your goals.

If you already have a clear, definable goal(s) in mind, you may feel you don't need to bother with the Life Circle. However, you may find it a useful and thought-provoking exercise and it may uncover for you some goals, perhaps not financial, that you had not recognised previously, or that you and your partner have not discussed.

Go to the SORTED! website at www.sortedfinancially.co.uk for up to date information and to download your free guide to current tax data.

7

Goal Setting

2

What is the value of money to you?

Money is only a tool which can be used, in one way or another, to buy what we want - be it a debt free existence, a yacht or a different lifestyle. What does money mean to you? Before you go any further, you need to work out your goals.

A serious business

Your beliefs and values about money may have been formed at an early age but now is the time to get them out, dust them off and re-examine them.

Think about what's important to you. This can go really deep. Dealing with your profound values and dreams may be difficult and there may be some pain around issues that impact the planning process. Persevere: it will be worth it!

Consider everything

All sorts of random ambitions, some deep and meaningful, some more trivial, may occur to you initially as goals when you first start thinking about it – jot them all down and don't expect all your serious goals to occur to you immediately. Give it one or two days, carry the list with you all the time and jot down any new goals that occur to you as you go along. Compare notes with your partner at every opportunity.

Go to the SORTED! website at www.sortedfinancially.co.uk for up to date information and to download your free guide to current tax data.

Open your mind

Your goals may not be directly financial: indeed, it is hoped that they will certainly not all be. However, inevitably there will be financial implications to most or all of the goals, such as a reduced income in early retirement, cost of further education courses, or the cost of buying a piano and lessons in order to become an expert performer of Rachmaninov.

Timescale

Each of your goals should have a timescale attached to it – repay credit card debt within one year, retire at age 63, fund for children's university costs starting in seven years' time, move to a larger house in four years' time, etc. Without the relevant timeframe, it is very difficult to know how much to fund for, or even to test whether you are achieving your goals.

Focus

You may now have a long list of goals. In order to create a plan for success, you need to whittle these down to a manageable few that you can focus on. Thinking about the following questions may help you to decide what goals are really important to you and to get the timescales into perspective:

Go to the SORTED! website at www.sortedfinancially.co.uk for up to date information and to download your free guide to current tax data.

10

> ➤ If you knew you would die tomorrow, what would you most regret not having done in your life?
> ➤ Similarly, if you knew your life would end in one year's time, what would you like to do most in the time available?
> ➤ If you knew that you had 10 years to live, what would you like to achieve in the years that you had remaining?

Reality Check

It may be that this whole process will spur you on to seek promotion, to change jobs or start your own business – in other words to manage an increase in your income. But, for most of us, results will be achieved by our own efforts in organisation and the discipline of saving or repaying debt. It is therefore very important that we are realistic about our goals.

This is especially important in this time of economic woes: many people have lost their jobs and it may be difficult for them to find new ones, at least until the economy picks up again. If you find yourself in this situation then, for the moment, your single goal may be to survive financially, to hang on to your house etc. This period may be one of great change for you and your family: your partner may become the bread winner or you may look to a completely new career. Either way, you are likely to have to be adaptable and well organised.

Whilst you are going through this difficult period, try not to lose sight of your long term goals: you should have these in mind when making any life decisions.

Go to the SORTED! website at www.sortedfinancially.co.uk for up to date information and to download your free guide to current tax data.

Even if your job is secure, you still need to be realistic. If you have three children, are earning £25,000pa, have a mortgage and no money in the bank, then no amount of reading this book or any other will enable you to buy a holiday villa in the Caribbean in two years' time. In order to see success in achieving goals, and therefore to have the momentum to continue to strive for them, they must be realistic.

In general, people over-estimate what they can achieve in the short term but under-estimate what they can achieve in the longer term. Be prepared for this process to be a long one if you have ambitious goals – and stick with it.

If your goal appears to be within the realms of reality then it stays on the list. If not, take it off.

How much will your goals cost to achieve?

To be realistic, we need to be able to put a cost on what it is we are trying to achieve. Take each goal, one by one, and calculate the amount of money you will need to be able to achieve them. Take note of the timescale for each goal.

There are a number of calculators available on various helpful websites: have a look at the SORTED! website for more information. These calculators will enable you to estimate, for instance, how much you will need to save each month in order to provide a specific sum at some time in the future or to provide a pension of a particular amount, from a certain age.

Go to the SORTED! website at www.sortedfinancially.co.uk for up to date information and to download your free guide to current tax data.

Guide only

Any calculations of this type that you make now will not be accurate and can only be a guide for the future: they inevitably rely on a number of assumptions. They are valuable nonetheless and give a framework to work within and also provide a reality check.

Inflation kills

Remember in doing any of these sums that inflation destroys value.

£1,000 will buy an awful lot more today than £1,000 will buy in 10 years' time – the rising cost of goods and services means we need to make an allowance for the decreasing value of our money, over time. On the plus side, for those who are still working, we might reasonably expect that, all being well, our earnings will increase over time to at least keep pace with price inflation – but this cannot be guaranteed.

It is also heartening to think that inflation works to effectively reduce the real value of capital debt that may be outstanding on mortgages or loans, over the years – the longer you have the mortgage, for instance, the more inflation will reduce the real value of the amount that you owe. *However*, the longer you have the mortgage, the more interest you will pay so there are swings and roundabouts!

When calculating the cost of each of your goals allow for inflation over the timescale for that goal. To do this, take the cost that you have calculated for the goal and multiply that

Go to the SORTED! website at www.sortedfinancially.co.uk for up to date information and to download your free guide to current tax data.

13

figure by, for instance, 1.04 for each year of the timescale. [This assumes an annual inflation rate of 4% - you can assume any rate that you feel is appropriate].

Shortlist

So now you have a shorter list of goals and objectives that you (and your partner if you have one) have agreed upon and you have calculated a very rough cost for each of your goals, making allowance for inflation.

Test your goals

As the final 'filter', go back to your Life Circle in Appendix 1 and 'test' each goal against it, one by one. If you were to achieve that goal, would that improve your 'score' in one or more areas of your life? If not, then forget it and concentrate on the goals that will improve the scores on your Life Circle. This will help you to shorten your list of goals even more to those that are really going to make a difference to your life.

Measuring success

It's important to be able to recognise success so, in respect of each of your short-listed goals, ask yourselves:

"What would have had to have happened in the next three / five / ten years (your timeframe) for you to feel that you had achieved your goal?"

Go to the SORTED! website at www.sortedfinancially.co.uk for up to date information and to download your free guide to current tax data.

14

If it isn't written down, it doesn't exist!

Record your final list of goals, including timeframes and the characteristics of success at the back of the book. Space is provided in Appendix 2. Separately, record the estimated cost of each goal. There are three versions available so that you can restate your goals, which may change as time goes by.

Go to the SORTED! website at www.sortedfinancially.co.uk for up to date information and to download your free guide to current tax data.

15

Motivation
Living life on purpose and taking responsibility 3

You are going to need to stay motivated in order to achieve your goals. This may not be as hard as you fear: once you start the process, you will immediately begin to feel the satisfaction of having taken control of the situation. There will be a momentum to that satisfaction which should carry you along over time.

To help you further, think about how you would feel in three / five / ten (your timeframe) years if you had achieved your goals? *Focus on that feeling.*

Be clear about what you want

It is said that 80% of achieving something is knowing *why* you are doing it because that's what gives you the motivation: only 20% is knowing *how* to do it. So, concentrate on the ultimate goal and that feeling that you'll have when you have achieved it and then, to a great extent, the rest will take care of itself.

You will find that you now have more purpose in your life – you are working towards something, or a number of things, that you have decided upon (jointly with your partner, if appropriate), in a positive way. You know you can achieve them.

With purpose comes responsibility – it is your responsibility to make the necessary changes happen in your life. Remember this and it will help you to stick to your principles and to maintain

Go to the SORTED! website at www.sortedfinancially.co.uk for up to date information and to download your free guide to current tax data.

17

the self-discipline that you will need. This of course applies in all sorts of areas of your life in just the same way – getting physically fit, for example.

Public commitment

Discuss your goals and the journey that you are embarking on, not only with your partner but with friends and family. They will help you stick to your plan in future – and just the fact that you have made that public commitment will be good discipline.

Don't be put off by negative comments from anybody: if they are not supportive, don't waste your time with them.

The cost of delay

'Time flies' is a common saying and for good reason. Procrastination has never been clever but in this context it could mean the difference between achieving your goals and not. Delay in starting to save or starting to reduce debt will have significant consequences which you may never be able to reverse.

If you really want to achieve your goals, start *NOW*.

Go to the SORTED! website at www.sortedfinancially.co.uk for up to date information and to download your free guide to current tax data.

18

Financial planning is a process – follow the six steps, in order, and you will get to where you want to be.

➤ Confirm goals and objectives

➤ Establish Net Worth statement

➤ Analyse income and expenditure

➤ Create strategies / plan

➤ Implement the plan

➤ Regularly review

Go to the SORTED! website at www.sortedfinancially.co.uk for up to date information and to download your free guide to current tax data.

Getting things sorted out
4

'Magpie' management

Many of us have a filing cabinet or a couple of desk drawers or even a few cardboard boxes full of papers relating to bank accounts, policies, investments or debts of one sort or another. Go on – admit it!

Some people seem incapable of throwing anything away, with the result that their lives are cluttered, literally and emotionally, with 'stuff' which is of no real value to them. This especially applies to paperwork.

Nothing can be achieved from this position: you will need to get everything sorted out before you can start to make a difference to your life.

What do all these pieces of paper relate to? What does it all mean? Often the financial arrangements that we have (bank accounts, loans, credit cards, policies, investments) all seemed like a good idea at the time, especially if accompanied by either an urgent need to find a quick fix to a problem or else the persuasive powers of a salesman. Are they relevant now and what is their significance?

We have let the direct debits go on and, not having the time to deal with the issue immediately, stuck the papers away without understanding them fully. We have stuffed the annual

Go to the SORTED! website at www.sortedfinancially.co.uk for up to date information and to download your free guide to current tax data.

21

statements or correspondence relating to these things in the same general area of our desk, filing cabinet or cardboard box(s), but possibly not in a meaningful way.

Make time to deal with this. Take a deep breath, get all the papers out and sort them so you know what piece of paper relates to what. Make a list of what these things are and take some time to read the literature that you are sorting. There may be something that you don't understand – in which case you may have to ring the provider and ask for an explanation – but the chances are that you have all you need in front of you to understand what you have. This will enable you to dispose of paperwork that you don't need and to gain a better understanding of your overall position.

Remember – make a list :

- ➤ What is it?
- ➤ What is it for?
- ➤ What does it cost?
- ➤ What is it worth / what do you owe?
- ➤ What commitment is there to future expenditure (loan payments / premiums)
- ➤ When will it end / mature?

This process will allow you to get a much better idea of the bigger picture of what you have.

Go to the SORTED! website at www.sortedfinancially.co.uk for up to date information and to download your free guide to current tax data.

Good feeling

No doubt you have been meaning to do this for ages, so the process will make you feel extremely good, especially when you have completed it.

Keep it up

It is important of course to maintain your paperwork in good order but if you are committed to your plan to succeed, this will come naturally.

Don't get carried away

A major part of the pleasure of this process lies in getting rid of lots of pieces of paper that have been clogging up your home and your life. That's great and you will feel really good about it but remember that if you are dealing with something that involves tax (income or capital gains) you should retain the essential records of purchase, income or capital receipts for a minimum period of six complete tax years as HMRC (HM Revenue & Customs) may require you to provide information about them. Perhaps you have the facility to scan the documents and store them on your computer: if so that's great and this would allow you to get rid of even more paper but do be sure that the data is secure and that you have a backup in case the computer packs up.

You should also retain a record of any gifts (amount, date and donee) that you have made, for inheritance tax purposes.

Go to the SORTED! website at www.sortedfinancially.co.uk for up to date information and to download your free guide to current tax data.

Identity Theft

Identity theft is a very real threat. Remember to destroy any paperwork that shows your name, address and details of any accounts or investments, very carefully before you put it in the recycling. Shred it!

Go to the SORTED! website at www.sortedfinancially.co.uk for up to date information and to download your free guide to current tax data.

24

Information is power

5

Net worth statement

This is exactly what it says it is – a statement of all your assets and liabilities. The difference between the two is your net worth, in financial terms. It is important to recognise that we are talking about financial terms here: just because your net assets may be very small, or even negative, this does not reflect on your worth as a person.

Assets

List *every* one of your financial assets of whatever kind and record a value. For liquid assets (readily realisable) this is likely to be bank accounts, deposit accounts, investments etc. You may need to make a couple of calls to find out the current values of some of your assets. Other assets may include your home, your yacht, works of art, your business etc. You may need to estimate a value for these investments: take care not to overestimate.

Record ownership for each item – yours, your partner's or joint.

Where it is possible to do so, record the rate of return that you are receiving on assets (eg interest on deposit accounts) as well as the accessibility (eg any notice period on the deposit account). This information will be useful later.

Go to the SORTED! website at www.sortedfinancially.co.uk for up to date information and to download your free guide to current tax data.

Pension plans

Under the heading of assets, you should record any pension scheme entitlements or personal pension plans that you have. These are not accessible, readily realisable assets but they may have a significant impact on your forward planning.

You will have been sent annual statements of your entitlement under your occupational scheme or an estimate of the benefits that your plan might provide and these would normally show a transfer value (the amount that the trustees would be prepared to transfer to another pension scheme in exchange for you giving up your entitlement from their scheme). Although this is a far from perfect measure, record the transfer value as the asset value in your net worth statement.

See the section on Retirement planning for more information on pension plans.

Liabilities

It's very important that you understand all your commitments.

List out *all* of your liabilities (what you owe), in detail, showing balances outstanding on each. This will include mortgages, personal loans, credit card balances, car loans/HP/lease commitments or bank overdrafts. Again, record ownership for each item – yours, your partner's or joint. You may need to make a few calls to get up-to-date balances for debts outstanding on mortgages and other borrowings.

Go to the SORTED! website at www.sortedfinancially.co.uk for up to date information and to download your free guide to current tax data.

26

Also record, for each of your liabilities, the monthly payments (if defined), the details of the interest you are paying, payment term and restrictions, if any, on early repayment. You may need this information later when developing strategies for reducing these debts.

Remember that if you have joint liabilities and for some reason your partner stops meeting their part of the commitment, you will almost certainly be responsible for the whole debt yourself.

Net Worth

For you and your partner combined, subtract your total liabilities from your total assets and this will give you your current combined net worth.

This is the figure that you are going to be aiming to improve in order to realise your objectives: it will provide a point of reference for the future.

Record the net worth statement, in as much detail as you can, in the back of the book in Appendix 3. There are three versions available so that you can record the updated situation when you are reviewing progress.

Go to the SORTED! website at www.sortedfinancially.co.uk for up to date information and to download your free guide to current tax data.

27

You are moving through the six step process, and getting closer to where you want to be.

- ➢ Confirm goals and objectives

- ➢ Establish Net Worth statement

- ➢ Analyse income and expenditure

- ➢ Create strategies / plan

- ➢ Implement the plan

- ➢ Regularly review

Go to the SORTED! website at www.sortedfinancially.co.uk for up to date information and to download your free guide to current tax data.

28

Income and expenditure analysis

Income

List out your net income from all sources. This list may include the following:

> ➢ Salary/self-employed earnings

> ➢ Pensions (state and/or private)

> ➢ Interest on cash deposits (bank/building society)

> ➢ Investment income (dividends or distributions from investments that you hold)

> ➢ State benefits (Job Seekers Allowance, Child Benefit, Incapacity Benefit, Attendance Allowance etc)

> ➢ Other income (this may include things such as income you are claiming under an insurance policy, child maintenance etc).

Remember that income from some investments and some state benefits (eg ISAs, some National Savings products, Attendance Allowance etc) are tax free.

If you receive a state pension, this is typically paid gross (ie without the deduction of income tax) but it is still taxable. It is assumed that the state pension will be set against your Personal

Go to the SORTED! website at www.sortedfinancially.co.uk for up to date information and to download your free guide to current tax data.

29

Allowance (the amount of income that you can enjoy each year before you have to pay any income tax) – but remember that there is still, potentially, liability to income tax.

If you are self-employed or do not have income tax deducted at the full rate from income (eg rental income), then make an allowance for this. If you are self-employed, you also potentially have liability to pay Class 4 National Insurance in addition to the small payments of Class 2 that you make: ask your accountant about this.

If you are a higher rate taxpayer then you will need to make allowance for the fact that you will also have higher rate tax to pay on most of your unearned income. For instance, interest on deposit accounts will have tax deducted at the basic rate but you will be liable to pay a further amount of higher rate tax.

If you are a very high earner your income may be subject to an additional rate of income tax and/or you may lose your entitlement to a personal allowance. If you are fortunate enough to fall into either category, you are advised to seek advice from a professional.

Tax Calculation

If your affairs are relatively simple, then the list of income (after tax) should be straightforward to put together.

If your affairs are more complicated and particularly if you are a higher rate taxpayer, you may have to do a calculation to understand your liability to income tax. You need to do this separately for you and your partner.

Go to the SORTED! website at www.sortedfinancially.co.uk for up to date information and to download your free guide to current tax data.

See the SORTED! website for information on rates and allowances.

Expenditure

This is the big one!

Analyse your expenditure

List, in as much detail as possible, an analysis of your normal expenditure on a monthly basis remembering to include an allowance for items that may only occur quarterly or once a year (eg holidays, car tax, insurance etc).

This is where you will need to make most effort and it may take a while but, be assured, the benefits will be enormous. This is where we all can learn most and many of us will be shocked at the amounts that we are spending on things that we may kid ourselves are not significant areas of expenditure.

Start with three months' bank statements (if you operate more than one current account then you will need to look at all of these and combine the information). This will tell you about regular outgoings, utilities etc. It will also throw up a large number of 'unrecognised' items – these are where you may need to refer to memory banks or receipts.

Think carefully about how you spend cash and be honest with yourself! Keep a note of every cash purchase you make (newspaper, coffee and so on) for a week – you will learn a lot.

Go to the SORTED! website at www.sortedfinancially.co.uk for up to date information and to download your free guide to current tax data.

Keeping receipts is very helpful – refer them back to the bank or credit card statements or use them to keep a check on what cash you are spending. This will give you a clearer idea of where your money is going. Do this *frequently*.

Software

There are some very reasonable (some are free) software packages available to help you accurately analyse your expenditure. These allow you to download your bank accounts and credit card statements from online banking and then analyse each item. If you bank online, try and get one of these packages.

Keeping it up to date

Once you have completed this onerous task, it will be much easier to keep it up to date in future and you will find it useful to do so. This is a big part of being in control and this knowledge will be empowering.

Income minus expenditure

Compare your joint, after-tax, income against your expenditure.

> ➢ What is the difference ?

> ➢ Is that difference positive or negative?

In order to be able to realise your dreams, you are probably going to need to change or improve this result. This will enable you to reduce debt, or save, as required.

Go to the SORTED! website at www.sortedfinancially.co.uk for up to date information and to download your free guide to current tax data.

32

Check your work

By looking at a combination of bank account balances and credit card balances at the end of each month, most people will be able to see the net effect of their combined income and expenditure. Does the combination of balances at the end of each month go up or down by approximately the same amount as the difference between income and expenditure you have recorded?

Use this as a check on whether you have been accurate in your analysis of income and expenditure – but remember that you may have to make allowance for some things such as where you are making minimum payments to the credit card each month, rather than clearing the debt. In this case, your payment to the credit card will not be a true reflection of what you have spent using that card.

Congratulations!

You have all your 'ducks in a row'.

The hard preparatory work that you have done on income and expenditure, particularly on analysing your expenditure, is enormously valuable and this is likely to hold the key to achieving your goals. Now you have put yourself in a position to start making a difference.

Go to the SORTED! website at www.sortedfinancially.co.uk for up to date information and to download your free guide to current tax data.

ACTION: Keep a careful, tidy note of all your analysis: these are records you may need to return to in future.

You are moving nicely through the six step process, and getting closer to where you want to be.

> Confirm goals and objectives

> Establish Net Worth statement

> Analyse income and expenditure ✓

> Create strategies / plan

> Implement the plan

> Regularly review

Go to the SORTED! website at www.sortedfinancially.co.uk for up to date information and to download your free guide to current tax data.

34

Last things first 6

Before we can begin on the exciting job of getting you moving towards your goal, there are a couple of important things that need to be done.

Wills

Do you (and your partner) have a will and is that will up to date and does it reflect all of your wishes as to how your estate should be distributed should you die tomorrow?

Have you or your partner been married, or divorced (including civil partnerships) since your wills were drawn up? If so, you may need a new will: the old one may be invalid.

Do you realise that if you die without having made a will, the way in which your assets are distributed will be dictated by a set of rules which may bear no relation to your wishes on the matter. In the extreme, your estate would pass to the Crown!

If you don't have a will, don't put it off any longer. It's particularly urgent if you and your partner are not married or not in a civil partnership: if you have children together and are not married a will is doubly important.

There is very much more to a will than dictating how your estate should be distributed: there is the issue of who should have control of those assets. For instance, if you are on your

Go to the SORTED! website at www.sortedfinancially.co.uk for up to date information and to download your free guide to current tax data.

second marriage and have minor children by your first, you may wish to leave money in trust for them until they are adult. You will need to appoint trustees to take care of that money on behalf of the children in the meantime. If you and your current spouse have children and you are considering the awful prospect that you both may die before the children are 18, you may wish to appoint guardians to take care of the children as well as trustees to take care of the money.

You will also need to appoint an executor(s) (or personal representative(s)) who will be responsible for the process of collection of your assets, settlement of your debts and distribution of your estate, in line with the instructions in your will, when the time comes. This could be the same person(s) that you appoint as trustees, somebody different that you feel is up to the job or a firm of solicitors (bear in mind solicitors' fees for this service can be significant).

When contemplating appointing trustees, guardians and executors, make sure that you consult with the individuals beforehand and that they are happy to take it on. It is not usually sensible to appoint people of a generation older than your own simply because, in the natural order of things, they are likely to die before you.

Keep your will up to date

Things change. Make sure that if there is a significant change in your life that affects how you might like your assets to be distributed or controlled after your death, you review your will.

Go to the SORTED! website at www.sortedfinancially.co.uk for up to date information and to download your free guide to current tax data.

36

Get more information and help

There is a lot of information available on line about wills and putting your affairs in order. Go to the SORTED! website for some suggested online resources.

Responsible action

Nobody enjoys making a will and thinking about what it means but it is important and need not take a long time or cost a huge amount. We are all going to die sometime and this is fundamental in getting your affairs sorted out and the peace of mind that that will bring you. So, don't put it off!

There are three ways of getting wills made:
- ➢ Through an appropriately qualified solicitor (this would always be the advised option, particularly if your affairs are anything other than very simple).
- ➢ There are will writing services which may be a little cheaper than using a solicitor but remember that they may not have the same level of qualification as a solicitor.
- ➢ You can buy a will writing kit (main stationery stores sell them) which enable you to write your own – there may be risks and this is not really advised but it is better than nothing.

Safekeeping

Keep your will in a safe place with other important papers (life assurance policies etc) and make sure that someone close to you (as well as your executor(s)) knows where it's kept.

Go to the SORTED! website at www.sortedfinancially.co.uk for up to date information and to download your free guide to current tax data.

Intestacy Rules

These rules apply where someone dies without having a valid will in place. Go to the SORTED! website for notes on these rules.

Powers of Attorney

While we are dealing with dread situations, consider what your position might be if you become incapable, for whatever reason, of managing your own affairs. This might be because you are physically or mentally incapable of doing so.

If you do not already have a Power of Attorney in place then, to address this situation, you need to have a Lasting Power of Attorney (LPA). There are two types of Power of Attorney: the first, the Property and Affairs LPA allows you to choose one or more people to make decisions on your behalf regarding your property and financial affairs should you lose the capacity to do so, or even lack confidence to do so, yourself.

The second type of LPA is a Personal Welfare LPA, by which you can name one or more people to make decisions on your behalf regarding your personal healthcare and welfare. This may involve the attorney making decisions about whether or not you continue to live in your own home or whether residential care would be more appropriate, if you are unfit to make these decisions yourself. It may also involve making decisions about your healthcare and medical treatments.

Go to the SORTED! website at www.sortedfinancially.co.uk for up to date information and to download your free guide to current tax data.

38

LPAs can only be brought into play after they have been registered with the Office of the Public Guardian so there is no risk that decisions will be taken out of your hands while you are still capable and still wish to make them yourself.

Be very careful to choose the right people for these roles: they should be people that you really trust, ideally be younger than you and, importantly, they should be prepared to take on the responsibility should the need arise.

Although you may feel that you are too young to be thinking about this, it is worthwhile discussing the matter with the solicitor when you are sorting out your will.

Inheritance Tax

Regulations relating to inheritance tax (IHT) change from time. Go to the SORTED! website for up to date information on allowances, rate of tax etc.

There are a number of ways in which IHT can be mitigated. If this is a big issue for you, take advice from a professional financial planner or a solicitor.

ACTION: Get your wills, guardians and powers of attorney (if applicable) sorted out now.

Go to the SORTED! website at www.sortedfinancially.co.uk for up to date information and to download your free guide to current tax data.

Protecting yourself and your family   7
'Expect the Unexpected'

Some benefits are provided by the state in the event of death, disability or long-term illness. Go to the SORTED! website for information about where to find the latest information on benefits.

If you have a partner or a family, it is vitally important that you consider their situation, as well as your own, in the event that you were to meet an untimely death or become disabled (possibly needing care) or unwell and unable to continue to earn at previous levels. It would be irresponsible to do anything else.

Even if you are single and don't have other people who are financially dependent on you, you should still consider what your situation would be if you were disabled by accident or illness and unable to work. Consider also the possibility that you contract a condition (physical or mental) that means you are unable to work, or unable to work at your usual occupation and forced to take a more lowly paid position. If you were to die, you would not be here to worry about it, but if you were disabled or longer term sick (statistically far more likely before age 65), you would most certainly be affected.

Life Assurance

The idea of life assurance is to provide financial security for your dependants, if you die. People are reluctant to think about

Go to the SORTED! website at www.sortedfinancially.co.uk for up to date information and to download your free guide to current tax data.

41

the possibility of death, especially when they are young, and as a consequence are often happier to part with premiums to insure their mobile phone than they are to pay to provide for their family in the event of their death. This is illogical!

Imagine the classic situation of husband (the breadwinner), wife and two small children. They have a mortgage on their house and a car loan. If he died tomorrow, with no life assurance, his family would be in a real mess. There would be some state benefits but certainly this would not enable the family to live in anything approaching the way in which they, or the deceased, would have liked them to. The widow would wish to pay off the mortgage and the car loan: in addition, she would need to provide for the daily needs of the growing family.

The cost of the widow and the children living in the same house would be not a lot less than the costs that there were when the husband was alive: a lot of the fixed costs of living (utilities, household insurance, running the car etc) would remain the same, although there would be some reduction in the food bill, leisure bills etc.

As the children grow older our widow may want to get a job, in which case she would be generating some income towards the costs of running the family and home. However, each situation is different and we cannot predict what the future will bring.

There are 2 basic types of life assurance policies available. These types are also available for critical illness policies with the exception of Family Income Benefit.

Go to the SORTED! website at www.sortedfinancially.co.uk for up to date information and to download your free guide to current tax data.

Term Assurance

Term assurance provides the cover for a fixed term (eg 25 years) and then stops. Term assurance policies are not usually renewable after the end of the term (although some renewable term assurance policies are available) and will not acquire a surrender value at any time.

The virtue of term assurance policies is that they are generally the cheapest form of cover and they are quite straightforward. The sum assured (cover) is payable on death within the term of the policy provided that premiums are paid when due. The appropriate term for such a policy will depend on the risk that is being covered: it may be the outstanding term of a mortgage, it may be until retirement age, it may be to cover the period during which your children are financially dependent or in private education and so on. It may be appropriate to have more than one policy with differing terms to cover different eventualities.

There are variations on the theme of term assurance which may be appropriate, for instance Family Income Benefit policy which, rather than providing a single lump sum of death of the insured, would instead provide an amount of money to the beneficiaries, each year for the unexpired term of the policy. This might be useful, for instance to cover private school fees where the cost and the number of years for which the fees are payable are known in advance.

Decreasing term assurance which may be useful to cover a repayment mortgage where the amount outstanding is decreasing over the term of the mortgage. Think about this

Go to the SORTED! website at www.sortedfinancially.co.uk for up to date information and to download your free guide to current tax data.

43

carefully though: most people increase their borrowing at some stage during their lives and in this case your decreasing term assurance may become inadequate.

Whole of life policies

These policies provide the reassurance that, once your initial application has been accepted by the underwriters, you will be able to maintain the cover for the whole of your life, no matter how your health may deteriorate. This means that, providing the premiums are maintained, the sum assured would be paid on death whether it be a week after the policy commenced or when you were 97.

There are various different kinds of these policies but, in the main, they are useful for specialist purposes and tend to be more expensive and complicated than term assurance policies.

How much life cover?

Deciding on the amount of life cover that is required is a difficult one. As a minimum, there should be sufficient to repay any debt (mortgage, loans, credit cards etc) and then on top of that there needs to be an amount sufficient to look after the family for a number of years, allowing for the surviving partner's earnings, if any. The appropriate number of years and the amount that should be allowed for each year will vary from case to case. It may be that a husband has another set of children from a previous marriage for whom he is also providing: covering this obligation would also need to be considered in a separate arrangement.

Go to the SORTED! website at www.sortedfinancially.co.uk for up to date information and to download your free guide to current tax data.

As a starting point, consider a minimum of the amount of any debts plus 10 times the difference between any continuing income of the survivor and the annual estimated cost of running the household without you, as being the amount of life cover that is sufficient. You might need this cover until your youngest child becomes independent.

In considering what the running cost of the household might be without you, always consider whether there would be any new costs, such as additional childcare that would have to be provided in order for your partner to manage.

The need for life cover in the event of a non-working spouse is often overlooked: consider that in our typical family scenario, if the wife were to die, the husband may be able to continue working but only if he can fund care for the children and housekeeping. He may not wish to leave his children with someone else, so he may decide that, for a period of years at least, he would prefer to look after them himself. In this case, there would need to be sufficient life cover on the mother's life to cover the widower's lost earnings.

Premiums

Life assurance premiums are lower the younger you are at the time of application, assuming you are in good health. If you delay taking out any insurance required, you should bear in mind that deterioration in your health could make you much more expensive to insure or, in extreme circumstances, uninsurable.

Go to the SORTED! website at www.sortedfinancially.co.uk for up to date information and to download your free guide to current tax data.

45

Inflation proofing

It may be appropriate, depending on the purpose for which you need the cover, to arrange a policy which provides a sum assured which increases each year in line with inflation, in return for an increasing premium. Look into the cost and try and find a policy where the premium increases at the same percentage rate as the level of sum assured.

Joint life policies

You and your partner will each need to consider the amount of cover that you need.

It is possible to arrange policies on a joint life basis, most usually joint life policies on a first death basis. This is where there is one policy which would pay out one sum assured when the first of the assured lives dies. Joint life, 'first death' term assurance policies can be very useful and may provide the very cheapest way of covering a specific risk but if you are considering this, also check out the cost of having 2 separate term assurance policies, one for each partner. The cost may be only a little more than a joint life policy and the arrangement potentially provides for 2 payouts (if both partners were to die within the term of their policies) as well as the additional flexibility of maintaining the second policy when either there is a claim on the first or where one or other becomes irrelevant.

Accidental death cover

You may be offered this type of policy by salespeople who may not go to great lengths to explain that a claim would only be met if death occurred as a result of an accident in certain

Go to the SORTED! website at www.sortedfinancially.co.uk for up to date information and to download your free guide to current tax data.

46

circumstances. This type of life cover is much cheaper than 'proper' life assurance but of little real value. If you need life cover, you need it, whatever the cause of death. If you possibly can, get 'proper' life cover: that is the only type that can give you peace of mind.

Critical Illness Cover

This type of cover is designed to provide a lump sum payment in the event that you are diagnosed with one of a large number of named conditions (eg. cancer, heart attack, stroke, MS and kidney failure plus many others). Typically, the person insured has to survive for a period of 28 days following diagnosis of the disease in order for the claim to be accepted. Critical illness insurance is very much more complicated than life insurance and you should be sure that you understand the circumstances in which a claim would be paid.

Often claimants are fit enough to return to work three or six months after the diagnosis.

Critical illness cover might typically be affected with a view to repaying the mortgage and other debts, possibly meeting the cost of converting a home to allow disabled living and also to provide a capital sum to cover the eventuality that the person affected is unable or unwilling to return to work.

Again this cover can be arranged on a term or a whole of life basis and policies often provide a combination of life assurance and critical illness cover. Critical illness cover is normally significantly more expensive than life assurance.

Go to the SORTED! website at www.sortedfinancially.co.uk for up to date information and to download your free guide to current tax data.

47

If you are taking out such a policy, make sure that it includes Total Permanent Disability cover. This means that if you contract some condition or suffer the effects of an accident which is not covered under the defined critical illnesses but still renders you permanently unable to return to work (or in some cases, to perform certain activities of daily living), the policy will still pay out. You should also check that this benefit becomes payable if you are rendered unable to continue your *own* occupation rather than *any* occupation, which would mean that the policy would not pay out if you were fit enough even to sell matches on the corner of the street.

Permanent Health Insurance / Income Protection Insurance

Income protection insurance provides an income benefit, commencing a specified time (the deferment period) after the onset of an illness or condition that prevents the insured person from working. The benefit is payable, provided that an assessor appointed by the insurer confirms that the insured person is unfit for work, until the earlier of death, reaching the expiry age of the policy (typically 60 or 65) or regaining health to the extent that he/she is deemed fit to return to work.

These policies provide an income and not a lump sum and often pay out in circumstances where a critical illness policy would not. The amount of the income that can be provided is usually limited to a percentage of your current earned income.

Go to the SORTED! website at www.sortedfinancially.co.uk for up to date information and to download your free guide to current tax data.

48

Because of the high incidence of long term absence from work due to ill-health, these policies are quite expensive. The longer the deferment period, the cheaper the insurance will be so if you are thinking about such a policy, plan to have an emergency fund which would carry you through until a later deferment date (perhaps one year) so that the policy would not start paying out until you had been ill for 12 months. This will reduce the premiums significantly but still provide cover for you and your family in the worst case.

Private Medical Insurance (PMI)

This is becoming more and more expensive and the costs increase quite dramatically with age, particularly in retirement when, of course, a claim is most likely. The cover may be provided for you (and your family) as an employee benefit though a group scheme: this may be 'free' although you would still be taxed on the cost of providing the benefit (as a Benefit in Kind) or you may be asked to pay for the cost of the cover for your family. The costs involved in a group scheme, such as an employer would offer, would typically be much lower than an individual policy and also would not necessarily exclude benefit in connection with any pre-existing conditions which most individual plans will.

Bear in mind that, for emergency or acute conditions (eg heart attack) the NHS still provides a very good service. The value of PMI is really for non-life-threatening conditions or where the insured simply wants to avoid general care and accommodation on NHS wards and to get things done at a time convenient to them.

Go to the SORTED! website at www.sortedfinancially.co.uk for up to date information and to download your free guide to current tax data.

For most of us who do not have PMI provided by our employers, it is a luxury.

Accident, Sickness and Redundancy insurance /Payment Protection plans

Whenever you have taken out a mortgage, loan, a credit card, finance terms for the purchase of a sofa, you are likely to have been encouraged to take out this insurance. It is a hugely lucrative market for the insurers and therefore for the people who are trying to sell it to you. Be wary!

The policy is supposed to meet your loan payments *for a limited time*, perhaps up to nine months, in the event that you are ill or suffer an accident and are not able to work for more than a month, or if you are made redundant.

This may sound attractive, especially the redundancy cover which cannot be accessed elsewhere – but just check out the restrictions and exclusions before you agree to it. Some of these policies exclude claims relating to conditions that you have ever suffered before or that could have been anticipated from illnesses that you have suffered before; some exclude stress, depression and back problems, as standard. Often, for the redundancy cover to be effective you have to have been continuously employed on a permanent contract by the same company for at least a year before you qualify.

Go to the SORTED! website at www.sortedfinancially.co.uk for up to date information and to download your free guide to current tax data.

50

The premiums are very high in relation to the potential benefits that are provided. Generally these policies are of very little value: if you feel the cover is of real benefit to you and you have understood all exclusions and the limit of the benefits, then go ahead, but do not allow yourself simply to be 'sold' a plan.

The best way to deal with these short term risks is to try to have an 'emergency' fund put by to cover outgoings for a period. If you aren't able to do this then you should ask yourself whether you should be taking the loan (to buy the sofa or whatever it may be), in the first place.

State of Health: Underwriting

Premiums quoted for any sort of life assurance, critical illness or income protection insurance, assume that you are in good health when you make your application. You will be asked to complete a health questionnaire. The insurer's underwriters will assess the answers you have given and may, depending on your answers, request either a report from your GP, a medical examination or, sometimes, blood tests. You will also be asked questions about your lifestyle, whether or not you are a smoker and whether you are involved in any high-risk pastimes or occupations (eg rock climbing, deep sea diving).

If you are in poor health, have suffered ill-health in the past or are a professional deep sea diver, you may find it more difficult – and certainly more expensive – to arrange cover.

Go to the SORTED! website at www.sortedfinancially.co.uk for up to date information and to download your free guide to current tax data.

51

Full disclosure

When completing any application for any type of insurance, never withhold information or include anything that is less than the full truth. If you do so, in the event of a claim, the insurer is entitled to decline the claim on the basis of non or false disclosure on the original application.

Your Right to Change Your Mind

If you feel you have been pressurised into buying any insurance product or indeed most investment plans, you have a right to change your mind and get a refund within 14 or 30 days of taking it out. Check out your rights.

Warning

When dealing with any kind of insurance, remember that the insurance company is not a charitable organisation: their interest is to maximise profits for their shareholders. They will not pay out claims on their policies unless they have to, so you need to understand any exclusions that are placed on the policy (eg. that a condition, such as back pain, is not covered by a permanent health insurance).

What cover do you need?

Before rushing into arranging new policies, think about what you really need.

Go to the SORTED! website at www.sortedfinancially.co.uk for up to date information and to download your free guide to current tax data.

Life assurance: is this relevant for you? If so:

> How much does there need to be available in the event of your death in order for you to feel that you have left your affairs in proper order and your family provided for?
> How much does there need to be available in the event of your partner's death in order for him/her to feel that they have left their affairs in proper order?
> How long is the cover required for?
> Does cover need to be increasing to keep pace with inflation?
> Would decreasing cover be suitable (eg to cover a capital and interest repayment mortgage or some other diminishing liability)?

Do you need Critical Illness cover? If so:
> How much does there need to be available in the event of you surviving diagnosis of a critical illness or total and permanent disability in order for you to have peace of mind?
> How much does there need to be available for your partner in the same circumstances?
> How long is the cover required for?
> Does cover need to be increasing to keep pace with inflation?
> Would decreasing cover be suitable?

Go to the SORTED! website at www.sortedfinancially.co.uk for up to date information and to download your free guide to current tax data.

53

Is PHI / Income Protection Cover appropriate to your situation? If so:

- ➤ How much monthly income would you need to provide for in the long term if you were prevented from returning to work (at your own occupation)?
- ➤ How much monthly income would your partner need to provide for in the long term if he/she were prevented from returning to work (at his/her own occupation)?
- ➤ How many months after the onset of illness would you need the benefits to start being paid?
- ➤ Until what age?
- ➤ Does the cover or the benefit (once in payment) need to be increasing to keep pace with inflation?

What do you already have?

Existing plans

Have a look through all of your existing protection policies (you will find this easy now that you have them all sorted): list out the benefits that they provide, length of cover and the cost.

Employee benefits

The benefits provided by some employers are very generous, which takes the pressure off us to provide the required life cover etc privately. This is great but, one word of warning: these days it is very unusual for employees to remain with the same employer in the long term. If you are completely dependent on your terms of employment to provide for your family in the event of your death or to help you in the event of ill-health, what will happen if you leave that employer and

Go to the SORTED! website at www.sortedfinancially.co.uk for up to date information and to download your free guide to current tax data.

54

move to another where the same level of benefits is not available?

Depending on the state of your health at the time that you change employer and your health history, it might prove difficult to obtain the insurance you need. For most of us this will be a calculated risk that we will live with but it might be sensible, even if there is a generous death benefit from your employment, to cover the fundamentals, such as your mortgage.

Sometimes, employers' employee benefit schemes will allow you to choose to some extent what benefits you have. In this case, consider the long term benefits: you are likely to need life cover and critical illness cover that extends beyond this employment and so, depending on your circumstances, it may be best to get the maximum employer pension contributions, income protection (in case of ill health) and private medical insurance and arrange your life and critical illness cover privately so that it will still be in place if you change employer.

If you are enrolled in an employer's group death in service scheme, you should be sure to complete an 'expression of wish' form to indicate who you would like the benefit to be paid to in the event of your death.

Go to the SORTED! website at www.sortedfinancially.co.uk for up to date information and to download your free guide to current tax data.

55

Make a list of all the protection benefits that your employer, if you have one, provides:

> ➤ Death in service benefit (check that your employer has your instruction to pay this to the correct person in the event of death)
> ➤ Critical Illness cover: this is less common but is provided by some employers.
> ➤ Income protection benefit: if you were to be ill in the long term, what percentage of your pay would your employer continue to pay you and for how long? (Remember that even if your employer does not provide a continuing income during absence due to ill health, you should still be entitled to Statutory Sick Pay)
> ➤ Private Medical Insurance

Other benefits

Don't forget to allow for death benefits payable under pension schemes/plans. If it is a personal pension plan, it is likely that a lump sum equal to the value of the fund at the time of death would be payable. (Check that you have nominated the correct person as being the one that you would wish to receive this benefit in the event of your death.)

An occupational pension scheme may provide a lump sum equal to the value of the fund or widow's, and possibly children's, pensions, depending on the type of scheme and the rules of the scheme.

Go to the SORTED! website at www.sortedfinancially.co.uk for up to date information and to download your free guide to current tax data.

56

Gap Analysis

Now that you know what you would like to have and what you have got, make a comparison between the two – a gap analysis.

> Is there a shortfall in the amount of the cover provided?
> Are the length of terms and the types of the existing policies/arrangements still appropriate?
> Have you got policies that you no longer need that are costing you money?

This will lead you to deciding whether you need to:

> Take on some additional plans
> Cancel unnecessary plans
> Cancel arrangements and replace them with new ones that provide more appropriate cover *

* If you are thinking of replacing plans, make sure that you have the cover under the new plans in place before you cancel the old ones. It may be that your state of health has deteriorated since you applied for your original plans and that you are no longer able to get normal insurance rates, so don't get rid of the old plans until the new ones have been accepted by the insurer. If it looks as if new plans will be very expensive, consider keeping the relevant existing plans and 'topping up' the cover with new plans rather than scrapping the old ones and starting again.

Before committing to new arrangements, consider the cost!

Go to the SORTED! website at www.sortedfinancially.co.uk for up to date information and to download your free guide to current tax data.

57

Don't over commit. You may have to consider reducing the cover to something less than the ideal: that will depend on your circumstances and what gives you peace of mind.

Getting Help

Professional help

If you are not being advised by a financial planner and your circumstances are complex, or you have health problems or are involved in hazardous pursuits, you should seek advice from an independent financial adviser (IFA), who will be able to advise you on the best type of policy, the level of cover and the insurer that will give you the best deal. If you can, get a recommendation from a friend to an IFA that they trust or else go to www.unbiased.co.uk and search by your local area. It may be that the IFA will receive commission from the product provider for arranging the policy or policies: this may be substantial and in this case there is a clear advantage in the adviser arranging larger policies. If you are in a position to do so, ask what it would cost if you were to pay a fee and have a policy with lower premiums that did not pay commission to the adviser.

Doing it yourself

You can easily buy life assurance online: there are a number of sites available that compare the premiums charged by different insurers for the same amount of cover. You can even do your application online. This is likely to be the quickest and cheapest solution, but you do need to be in reasonable health and know what you want before it becomes practicable. You also need to

Go to the SORTED! website at www.sortedfinancially.co.uk for up to date information and to download your free guide to current tax data.

58

be prepared to invest time to read about the possible additional benefits that may be included (eg premium protection cover, which provides for premiums to be effectively waived if you are not able to work for a period of time for reasons of accident or ill-health).

ACTION: Write down what you think you need to do to ensure that you have appropriate cover for yourself and your loved ones: then make the necessary arrangements.

Making progress

Well done for working your way through that lot! It may have been a bore but, it was important – and now that you have your plans sorted out to take care of the unexpected, you can move forward to the next stage, confident that you 'have it covered'.

Any money that you apply to these ends is not wasted and should not be thought of as such.

Now you can begin making a difference!

Go to the SORTED! website at www.sortedfinancially.co.uk for up to date information and to download your free guide to current tax data.

59

Retirement planning 8

Planning for retirement is one element of financial planning and not really a separate subject, but because of its complexity and importance, it warrants a section of its own.

Retirement planning shouldn't be thought of only in terms of pension schemes or plans. Pensions form an important, if a little complicated, part but are by no means the whole picture.

The length of time that the average person will spend in retirement is now projected to be between 25 and 30 years – potentially one third of our entire lives. The Government Actuaries Department have predicted that, by 2025, more than a third of the UK population will be over 55 and there will be more people over 60 than under 25.

We are told that someone aged 55 today has a one in two chance of living beyond age 90 and a one in four chance of living beyond age 95.

This represents a huge challenge for us as individuals and for society as a whole. In future the 'shape' of our society will be different and social attitudes, leisure facilities, care facilities for the elderly and the health service will all need to adapt. For the Government, as well as for us as individuals, the funding of these long periods of retirement also represents an enormous challenge.

Go to the SORTED! website at www.sortedfinancially.co.uk for up to date information and to download your free guide to current tax data.

61

How are we going to marshal all our financial resources to carry us through this long retirement period? It will require some planning. Leaving it until a few years before you expect to retire is not going to work!

Young people should be starting their pension provision as soon as they begin permanent employment even if they also have student debt to repay. This seems particularly harsh when earlier generations were able to take a more relaxed attitude: they could look forward to a living income being provided by the state and expected their employers to provide for them through generously funded final salary scheme pensions. But, harsh or not, it is a reality and everyone should take it seriously.

For older people, planning for retirement is about much more than paying into a pension plan. We all need to plan how all our financial resources can be employed to prepare for our retirement – possibly including the repayment of debts which our reduced income in retirement will almost certainly not support.

We also need to prepare in other ways for retirement: what are we going to do when we no longer go to work? How are we going to occupy our minds and keep our bodies in good enough condition to be able to realise our ambitions? It's all up to you.

When do you plan to retire? Do you plan to work part time for a while before giving up work completely? There is no longer a default retirement age (previously 65) which means that, in

Go to the SORTED! website at www.sortedfinancially.co.uk for up to date information and to download your free guide to current tax data.

62

most cases, your employer cannot force your retirement at any age provided you are still able to do the job.

For you, retirement may tie in with your major goal, for others the whole thing may seem much farther off. But whatever your age or circumstances, please do not try to convince yourself that you don't need to think about it yet. This is an area where the detrimental effect of the 'cost of delay' is enormous: start now.

The Government has recognised the problems ahead and legislation is changing to help/encourage/force people to make some provision for their retirement and to force employers to contribute too. Within a few years, it will be automatic for employees to be enrolled in their employer's pension scheme and for minimum contribution levels to be paid by both employee and employer. There will be an annual option to opt out of the arrangement but think very carefully before doing it: in most cases this would be foolish.

What do you have already?

'Private' pension schemes
If you already have some pension plans or preserved entitlements from current or previous employers' pension schemes, list them all out. Make sure that you understand your entitlement.

Are you entitled to a defined benefit from an employer's pension scheme? If so, how much is payable, and from what date? Does it increase once it is in payment and/or between

Go to the SORTED! website at www.sortedfinancially.co.uk for up to date information and to download your free guide to current tax data.

63

now and retirement age? Does it provide for a dependant's pension should your partner survive you?

Do you have a personal pension or money purchase employer's pension? These are known as defined contribution schemes and are very much less predictable in terms of what they will provide in future. They will have a current fund value and you should have been given an illustration of what pension this *might* provide at the selected retirement age. These figures are not in any way guaranteed but, for this purpose, will give you a rough idea of how much your income from pension plans might be. Does that illustration allow for your pension income to increase to keep pace with inflation?

In every case, make sure you understand the benefits that would be payable in the event of your death, both before retirement and after retirement date. This will vary from scheme to scheme and plan to plan. If you don't understand something, you may have to phone your HR department, the insurance company or the financial adviser that originally arranged the plan – it will be worth the effort involved.

State pensions

Remember that you will also, almost certainly, be entitled to a pension from the state. To discover what your entitlement from the state will be, you can request a projection from the Pensions Service. Go to www.direct.gov.uk for more information: once you have registered you will be able to get instant, online projections. It is important to try and understand what your entitlement will be and from what age you will receive it.

Go to the SORTED! website at www.sortedfinancially.co.uk for up to date information and to download your free guide to current tax data.

The question as to whether you will be able to claim the 'full' basic state pension will depend upon your national insurance contribution record, how many credits you may be entitled to for years caring for children and a number of other factors. However, the rules are changing and in future, your entitlement may depend not on your national insurance contribution record but on the number of years that you have been a resident in UK.

State pensions rise each year to stay in line, to some extent at least, with increases in the cost of living.

State pensions are also subject to income tax although they are usually paid without deduction of tax because it is assumed that the income will be set against your annual personal allowance – the amount of income you can enjoy without tax.

In addition to the basic state pension, you may be entitled to an additional state pension which arises from membership of SERPS (state earnings related pension scheme) prior to 2002 and/or S2P (state second pension) from 2002 onwards. As the names suggest, these entitlements are linked to the level of your earnings: you will need to obtain a projection of your state pension benefits in order to understand your entitlement, if any.

It may be that you have 'contracted out' of SERPS and/or S2P in the past, in which case you will not have a state pension entitlement from these schemes for the period for which you were contracted out but instead, in lieu of entitlement under these state schemes, you will either have a personal pension

Go to the SORTED! website at www.sortedfinancially.co.uk for up to date information and to download your free guide to current tax data.

65

plan which has been funded by contributions from HMRC or you will have paid lower national insurance contributions if you are a member of a contracted out occupational pension scheme. Contracting out of S2P will cease with effect from April 2012 for everyone other than those in defined benefit (final salary) occupational pension schemes.

State pensions are payable from state pension age which used to be 65 for men and 60 for women. The state pension age for women is rising gradually from 60 to 65: this will be complete by November 2018. Current rules provide for state pension age to increase from 65 to 68, for men and women, by 2046. These planned changes are in flux at the time of writing: for more information and a state pension age calculator, visit www.direct.gov.uk and search for state pension age.

The future of state pensions is difficult to fathom as the schemes are unfunded and the Government faces a real challenge. State pension schemes rely upon the receipts of national insurance contributions from the working population this week to fund the payments to pensioners next week. As the population ages, the number of people in work and paying national insurance relative to the number who are retired and drawing benefits is set to decrease at an alarming rate. The Government is trying to address this by restructuring benefits and extending the state pension age.

For those on very low incomes in retirement and who have very little capital there is, and will continue to be, some sort of minimum income provided, whether this takes the form of additional benefits or the whether the Government increase the

Go to the SORTED! website at www.sortedfinancially.co.uk for up to date information and to download your free guide to current tax data.

66

basis state pension for everybody to a level which should be sufficient to support anybody. However, please do not imagine that the level of income that the state will be able to provide will be sufficient to enjoy the sort of retirement to which you might aspire and also remember that it may not be payable until well after the age at which you would like to retire from work. Do not depend on it as your sole provision.

The option exists to put off taking your state pension if you are still working when you reach state pension age. In return for deferring the start date of your pension you will be entitled either to an increased pension or to a taxable lump sum, as you choose.

Remember that rules and state benefit structures may be subject to change and, if you can possibly make your own provision for a comfortable retirement, you should do so: it is very unlikely that the Government will be able to support you in any degree of comfort in future.

What is your target pension income?

Bearing in mind the analysis of your expenditure and thinking about how this might be different in retirement, you will be able to work out an estimate of the income that you will need after you stop earning. This will be very approximate, but it is a start.

Go to the SORTED! website at www.sortedfinancially.co.uk for up to date information and to download your free guide to current tax data.

67

What's the difference?

Do the gap analysis – subtract the amount that you estimate that you will receive from the state and any private pension arrangements you have, from your target pension income. This will give you a very rough idea of the projected income shortfall figure – you will need to fill this by additional pension contributions in the future or from other investments or assets.

You may be planning to move to a smaller home when you retire, thereby releasing capital – if so, include this in your calculations.

Remember to think carefully about your intended retirement age. If this is earlier than the retirement age selected for your existing pension arrangements, the benefits available to you will be reduced. State pension benefits will not be available before your state pension age although you can defer taking state pension benefits beyond your state pension age in return for a higher weekly benefit or a taxable lump sum.

Remember to think also about the effects of inflation. State pensions are 'inflation-proofed' to some extent but be careful when looking at projections from your private pension plans that they allow for inflation and the figures quoted are in 'real' terms. This is particularly important in retirement planning.

You will need to do some sums to calculate how much you would need to save each month to fund the shortfall. See the SORTED! website for direction to calculators that will help you.

Go to the SORTED! website at www.sortedfinancially.co.uk for up to date information and to download your free guide to current tax data.

68

ACTION: Make a note of the estimated cost of your retirement goal: you will need this when you are working out your financial plan.

General principles of pension planning

Pension planning remains complex despite Government efforts at simplification. See the SORTED! website for information about limits on tax relief on pension contributions and the limit on the total value of pension funds that an individual can have without tax penalties. These limits are unlikely to affect anyone reading this book but if you think you may be affected you should seek professional advice.

The basics that you need to understand are these:

Tax efficiency

Personal pension contributions are highly tax efficient because income tax relief is available on the contributions (within the limits) that you pay to a recognised pension plan. This means that the government will give back the income tax that you would otherwise have paid on the amount that you put into your pension plan.

This means that it actually costs you, in reduced take home pay, £80 to put £100 into your pension scheme if you are a basic rate taxpayer. If you are a higher rate taxpayer, more tax relief is available.

Go to the SORTED! website at www.sortedfinancially.co.uk for up to date information and to download your free guide to current tax data.

69

Employer contributions

Think of employer pension contributions as additional pay albeit restricted in the way that it is paid to you: do not undervalue this benefit.

If you have an employer who contributes to a pension scheme on your behalf, the amount that they contribute will vary according to the type of scheme that you have and the generosity of your employer. If you are one of the rapidly shrinking number of privileged people who are members of a defined benefit (final salary) scheme then your employer may be contributing a very large amount in order to cover the cost of providing your defined benefit in retirement. If you have a personal pension or a money purchase occupational pension scheme, your employer will be contributing a defined amount of contribution usually expressed as a percentage of salary. Let us assume that your employer matches your contribution rate to your pension scheme – this effectively means that, if you are a basic rate taxpayer, it will cost you £80 (in terms of take home pay) to get £200 into your pension pot: this is attractive!

Tax advantaged fund growth

If you are lucky enough to have a defined benefit pension entitlement, this will not be your concern but for those with defined contribution schemes, the fact that funds within an approved pension arrangement suffer very little tax is attractive. This means that the investment grows faster than it would otherwise.

Go to the SORTED! website at www.sortedfinancially.co.uk for up to date information and to download your free guide to current tax data.

70

Drawbacks

As with most things in life, there's a catch. The catch with pensions is that the timing and form in which benefits can be taken are restricted by legislation. In normal circumstances:

➤ No benefits can be taken before age 55.

➤ At the time that benefits are first taken, an amount is available as a lump sum payment which is paid tax free. For defined benefit schemes, this lump sum amount will be defined by the scheme rules but for defined contribution schemes, this would normally be a maximum of 25% of the total pension fund available at the time.

➤ The balance of any benefits from the pension arrangement must be used to provide an income for the rest of the member's life which will be taxed as earned income under PAYE.

Scheme rules

The rules of your employer's scheme, if you have one, will overlay the legislative restrictions above to dictate the retirement age and so on. Look carefully at any literature you are given about your pension scheme.

There is no doubt that defined benefit pension schemes are much more attractive to the member than defined contribution schemes. With the former the employer (or we, the UK taxpayers in the case of public sector schemes) takes the strain

Go to the SORTED! website at www.sortedfinancially.co.uk for up to date information and to download your free guide to current tax data.

71

of making up the difference in cost of the benefit over and above what the employee pays. In a defined contribution scheme, of whatever type, the member will have a pension fund at the benefit date the value of which cannot be predicted in advance as it depends upon investment performance as well as other factors. The rate at which the pension fund converts to income each year is another unknown. It is therefore very difficult to predict what benefits might ultimately arise for the member. For most people, there are a lot of different options available at the point of taking benefits and if you are unsure, you should seek independent advice about which would be best for you when the time comes.

Despite the unpredictability of benefits arising from defined contribution schemes, the tax treatment of contributions, the tax-advantaged growth of pension funds and the possibility of an employer pension contribution still make them attractive for most people. Because benefits are not allowed before age 55, pension plans also provide a disciplined way of saving for later life.

Conclusion

If you are employed or self-employed and you do not have a pension plan, you should seriously consider getting one unless your earnings or profit are very low. If your employer offers a scheme and also offers an employer contribution then you should probably join the scheme at the earliest opportunity. Try to make at least the level of personal contributions that will entitle you to the maximum employer contribution available under the arrangement.

Go to the SORTED! website at www.sortedfinancially.co.uk for up to date information and to download your free guide to current tax data.

72

If you are self-employed, the attractiveness of a pension arrangement will depend upon the level of income tax relief that you would get and how much you could afford to contribute. If your profits are low, you might prefer to have the flexibility of saving through ISAs or other taxable investments, in addition or as an alternative method of providing for your retirement. Either way, start as soon as possible.

ACTION: Make sure that all of your findings are recorded in a way that will allow you to come back to them. Allow for any pension contributions that you are making or intend to start making in your planned income and expenditure.

Getting help

This book does not seek to give specific advice on pensions – everyone's situation is different and the subject is complex. If you can't find the information you need on one of the many money websites and need advice, ask a suitably qualified financial planner or independent financial adviser. If you are a member of an occupational pension scheme, your HR department should be able to give you full information about your entitlement.

Go to the SORTED! website at www.sortedfinancially.co.uk for up to date information and to download your free guide to current tax data.

73

Budgeting
Planning your income and expenditure

9

Some 150 years ago, Charles Dickens wrote the following in his book 'Great Expectations'

> *'We spent as much money as we could and got as little for it as people could make up their minds to give us. We were always more or less miserable, and most of our acquaintance were in the same condition. There was a gay fiction among us that we were constantly enjoying ourselves, and a skeleton truth that we never did. To the best of my belief, our case was in the last aspect a rather common one.'*

The passage refers to the experience of the character in his late twenties but today this could be applied to a much broader age group.

The key to success in achieving your goals is increasing your disposable income. Get your spending under control and, if possible, also increase your after-tax income. This way you will have more available to apply to making your dreams happen.

You have made the first huge step towards controlling your expenditure by analysing what you spend your money on. You will already have some ideas about where you can improve the situation.

Go to the SORTED! website at www.sortedfinancially.co.uk for up to date information and to download your free guide to current tax data.

75

We are surrounded by warnings about the dangers of smoking, drinking to excess, obesity and so on – perhaps because these all have significant cost implications for the NHS. Where are the warnings about overspending, borrowing beyond a sensible limit and not making sufficient provision for your retirement? Although everyone is suffering in one way or another from the effects of the recession which came about, in part, as a result of uncontrolled borrowing and spending on the part of ordinary individuals as well as Governments, there is still too little advice given to the public. The Government does provide the Money Advice Service which you may find useful: check out their website. The Financial Planning Week website has a lot of tips to help you out and you will find some in the following pages.

We are all tempted by bingeing – binge drinking, binge eating and … binge spending. The first two of these can seriously damage your physical health, the third can seriously damage your financial health and the consequences for the future can be far-reaching. The need to repay debt, poor credit rating, and the inability to save can all put a blight on your future and barriers in the way of achieving your goals.

Go to the SORTED! website at www.sortedfinancially.co.uk for up to date information and to download your free guide to current tax data.

76

We are more likely to binge, in whatever way, if we haven't worked out our goals and are drifting along without purpose.

So, take a deep breath and PAUSE to give yourself time to take stock of what you are doing and where you are heading with it. It may be that you need to 'dry out' or cut down on eating and increase exercise or simply reduce your 'aimless' spending. Whatever it is, you need to take control of the situation!

You now have the advantage of having worked out what's important to you and identified your specific goals, which should make the task of taking control easier.

As with diet and exercise – where burning more calories than you are taking in as food will result in a loss of weight – so with budgeting, where an excess of income over expenditure will lead to an increase in net worth by reducing debt and increasing assets. The analogy goes further: depending on their metabolism, some people can lose weight easily and quickly while others battle for weeks on a couple of lettuce leaves to achieve the loss of a few pounds. It works the same way with

Go to the SORTED! website at www.sortedfinancially.co.uk for up to date information and to download your free guide to current tax data.

77

budgeting because some people simply have more to play with – higher income, smaller mortgage, one child instead of four and so on. Progress for some will be quicker than for others but the results are worthwhile, whatever the timescale. Remember, if the end goal is worth having, it is worth fighting for.

Think about everything that you spend

Obviously there are some essential things that must be paid (rent/mortgage, loan payments, community charge, tax, insurances, essential food, etc) but there is an awful lot of expenditure that is 'discretionary'. This applies equally to buying 'things' and spending money in the pub or at the coffee shop. Think about this very carefully – is the service or product that you are buying contributing to achievement of your goals and objectives in life? If not, do you need to spend that money or could you make different choices which would cost less or indeed nothing.

Some ideas for you to think about

Car boot sale – a one-off win

To get you started, why not do a car boot sale? While you are getting your financial world sorted, why not sort out the loft, the wardrobe, the garage or wherever you stash your (forgive the expression) 'junk'. You are a very unusual person if you aren't harbouring a lot of stuff that you will never need and which just might be of use to someone else. The chances are that if you haven't used something for 12 months, you never will – so get rid of it. It's a double win: not only do you gain space

Go to the SORTED! website at www.sortedfinancially.co.uk for up to date information and to download your free guide to current tax data.

and the satisfaction of having a more ordered home, but people may actually give you money for the stuff!

If you have anything left over that hasn't sold, do NOT take it home. Sort it out, there and then, into 'charity shop' or 'dump' and deliver it to it's new home immediately. Don't let it back in the house or it will surely find its way back into the loft, wardrobe or wherever!

Increasing income

> You could look for a higher paid job or seek promotion: if this is a possibility for you then go for it. In the present economic slump most people are happy to have a job at all, if they have one, but nevertheless there are still some opportunities for advancement.

> Some people are in a position to take on an extra job at weekends or evenings – perhaps something completely different from their 'day job'. Again, in current times there may be a lot of competition for part time jobs but this still may be a possibility for you.

> Rent a room. If you have a spare room and if such an arrangement could fit in with your life, you could let a room to increase your income. HMRC allows you to receive rent of up to £4,250pa, tax free, for letting out a furnished room in your house.

> State benefits. If you have not already done so, check that you are receiving all the state benefits that you are entitled to. Go to www.direct.gov.uk for information and direction to different departments. The Citizen's Advice Bureau and organisations like Age UK can also help and you should be able to find leaflets about

Go to the SORTED! website at www.sortedfinancially.co.uk for up to date information and to download your free guide to current tax data.

79

various different benefits at the Post Office. State benefits can make a big difference, particularly for families with children: we have all paid for them and they are our entitlement so don't think twice about claiming them. There is a shocking amount of Benefit Fraud going on in the UK and I would not wish to encourage anybody to add to that but, if your situation is genuine, the barrier of applying is well worth overcoming, particularly if you are having trouble making ends meet.

Keeping tabs on expenditure

If you are going to take control of your expenditure, a good first step is to make sure that you are either spending money in cash (keep the receipts for analysis) or else restricting your spending to the use of your debit card or, if necessary, a single credit card that you can, hopefully, repay at the end of each month. This will make it very much easier for you to track your spending and be the first step to getting things in order.

Keep good records on a spreadsheet or in a notebook: by recording your spending, you'll get a clearer idea of where savings could be made.

Controlling expenditure

It is often easier to pay a lot for something than to achieve the same result at a lower cost (eg eating out rather than cooking at home or 'getting a man in' to do the decorating rather than doing it yourself). Is eating out necessarily more enjoyable, healthier or a better use of your time than cooking at home?

Go to the SORTED! website at www.sortedfinancially.co.uk for up to date information and to download your free guide to current tax data.

80

Will the decorator come when he says he will and will he necessarily do a better job than you could have done? Often the answer to these questions is NO!

You will probably have more fun inviting friends to eat with you at home and developing your cooking skills! You will almost certainly feel enormous satisfaction at having done the decorating yourself!

Once you have worked out your objectives and what you really want to achieve in life, the chances are that you will worry less about surrounding yourself with 'things' to project an image. Instead you will project an image of someone who is focussed on success and has purpose, and you may no longer feel the need to buy so many clothes or accessories or gadgets. You may decide that it is better for you to walk than take a taxi.

Children

This is a difficult area – our kids exist in a competitive, materialistic world where commercial pressures encourage them to judge their own worth and that of others by the clothes they wear and the toys or gadgets they own. But these things do not add to your child's quality of life and they may not even enjoy them that much. We all have to find our own way of dealing with this problem and although you may not be able to eradicate it entirely, you can make a difference.

Be firm with the children, explain to them that there are more important things that your money should be spent on: encourage them to be individuals and to value more important

Go to the SORTED! website at www.sortedfinancially.co.uk for up to date information and to download your free guide to current tax data.

81

things than a new pair of designer trainers. Give them more of your time – much more rewarding for everyone.

While encouraging our children to look beyond the instant gratification of the latest 'must-have' we can do the same for ourselves. Remember what is really important to you and apply your energies (and your cash) to those things.

Practical ideas for saving money

This list is obviously not exhaustive but it may help:

Redundant outgoings

The analysis of your expenditure may have revealed some regular payments that you had forgotten about and that you could simply do without. Are you paying a gym subscription and no longer using the gym? Going through a list of all the direct debit and standing order mandates that are live on your current account(s) may reveal something that you don't need.

Food shopping

Before you go to the supermarket, make a shopping list (you know - like your mother or grandmother used to do!) and stick to it: don't let other items that you don't really need jump into your trolley. Online shopping as offered by the big supermarkets can be a good discipline and has the bonus that you don't have the hassle of visiting the supermarket yourself.

Go to the SORTED! website at www.sortedfinancially.co.uk for up to date information and to download your free guide to current tax data.

82

Eating out

Eat out less; eat at home more.

Going to the pub

Try to restrict the number of times that you go to the pub. Drinks bought in pubs and restaurants are expensive! Rather than miss the opportunity to meet up with your friends, why not invite them to your home one night a week?

Jobs around the home

If you are able to do it yourself rather than pay someone else to do it, then do.

Lunches

Not an original idea, but an effective one. If you habitually buy lunch every day at work, you could save pounds every day by taking a packed lunch instead. It also means that you can have whatever you like to eat and drink.

Smoking

If you are a smoker, you know what you need to do.

Quite apart from the damage to your health and the anti-social aspects, you could save well over £2000 a year if you smoke 20 a day.

Go to the SORTED! website at www.sortedfinancially.co.uk for up to date information and to download your free guide to current tax data.

83

Rent

If you are prepared to move, investigate how much you could save by moving to a different property. A smaller property might provide a saving in rental as well as cheaper council tax and utility bills. If you find somewhere nearer your place of work, you may reduce travel time and cost. Sharing the rent with someone else may also be a possibility if you have the necessary space and temperament.

Mortgage

If you have a mortgage, check that the deal that you have is the best for you/ cheapest available. Bear in mind that there are potentially considerable costs involved in re-mortgaging which could negate any other savings for a number of years. Nevertheless it is worth at least checking with your current lender that you are on the best deal that they can offer you. If your mortgage is large it may be worthwhile asking an independent Mortgage Broker if they are able to arrange a better deal for you or at the very least, checking some of the comparison websites to see what is available elsewhere.

If you are a higher rate taxpayer and you have cash savings, an Offset mortgage is worthy of consideration.

Remember that if you are a homeowner, the costs of moving home may be prohibitive: estate agent's fees, solicitor's fees, stamp duty and removal costs may wipe out potential savings.

Go to the SORTED! website at www.sortedfinancially.co.uk for up to date information and to download your free guide to current tax data.

84

Council tax

There are exemptions or discounts available for a number of classes of people. If you fall into one of the following categories, you may be eligible:

> ➢ If you are disabled
> ➢ If you are a carer looking after a disabled person
> ➢ If you are a student
> ➢ If you are an apprentice
> ➢ If you are a student nurse

If you are living on a very low income, you may be eligible for council tax benefit. Check with your local council or go to www.direct.gov.uk to find out more.

Cars

This is a big one, especially for the men. You may be in the habit of justifying to yourself the purchase of a new car every couple of years – but just think about this cost, and ask yourself whether it is helping you to achieve your objectives. The moment that you drive a new car out of the showroom, you lose about 20% of the money that you paid for it – whether it be a cash purchase or on credit terms. It's crazy! The people who are really laughing are those that buy the car from you after two years and get a bargain at your expense. Modern cars are reliable and should last for years: stick with what you have a bit longer, take care of it and save money.

The cost of running a car continues to spiral: if you are a two car family, think carefully about how you might be able to

Go to the SORTED! website at www.sortedfinancially.co.uk for up to date information and to download your free guide to current tax data.

85

manage with one so that you could apply the money saved towards your goals. Try at least to reduce the use of the car for short journeys (saving on fuel, parking costs and wear and tear) by walking more, using a bike or taking a bus. A scooter may be a much cheaper and viable alternative to a car for short journeys to work. Car-sharing is catching on for travel to work – is there a local scheme you could get involved with?

Try to avoid getting involved in car leasing arrangements unless you only need a car for a few years.

Clothes and fashion items

This is more aimed at the women. Do you really need those new clothes or accessories? Do you want them more than you want to achieve your goals?

Utility bills

These are now an increasing part of all our household costs and look likely to continue to be in future. You can compare gas and electricity prices from different suppliers on various comparison websites and there is useful advice available from the Office of Gas and Electricity Markets (Ofgem): check out their website.

> ➢ There are obvious practical steps that we could all take to reduce utility bills. Make sure your home is well insulated: you may be eligible for a grant that will cover the majority of the cost of insulation - check it out online.

Go to the SORTED! website at www.sortedfinancially.co.uk for up to date information and to download your free guide to current tax data.

86

> ➢ Reduce the temperature on your central heating thermostat by a few degrees and be prepared to wear a sweater around the house,
> ➢ Turn off the lights when you are not in a room and
> ➢ Turn off electrical appliances, including televisions and entertainment systems, rather than leaving them on standby.

If you are having difficulty heating your home or paying your utility bills and need help, you can call the Home Heat Helpline. Here you can get help and advice on identifying energy efficiency grants, arranging alternative payment methods, carrying out benefits checks and receiving specialist advice.

If you don't have a water meter fitted in your home and you are a moderate user of water, consider getting a meter fitted. You could save a lot.

Holidays

Many of us have become accustomed to spending a lot on holidays, perhaps travelling to exotic locations. Is this moving you towards your long term objectives? Could you have just as much fun and relaxation holidaying closer to home, perhaps camping with friends who are also trying to save money? If you discuss your goals with your friends, you may find they are thinking along the same lines and you could work together.

Insurances

When your general insurances (household, car etc) come up for renewal, check whether you could get the same cover cheaper

Go to the SORTED! website at www.sortedfinancially.co.uk for up to date information and to download your free guide to current tax data.

87

elsewhere. Try the online comparison sites. Also make sure there is no potential for saving on life insurance etc. – see chapter 7.

Public transport

If you are planning to make a long journey by train, book well ahead and be prepared to stick to specific trains. The cost of train travel can be prohibitively high in some cases but it is still possible to find some real bargains by booking early. Bear in mind that, generally, travel by long distance bus is cheaper than train travel.

Don't forget that for certain people there are valuable discounts available:

- ➢ Free off peak bus passes for those over the state pension age for women
- ➢ Railcards (need to be purchased) to provide discounted travel for over 60s, young people, family groups and the disabled.
- ➢ A special system exists for residents of London boroughs which covers rail, bus and underground.

Mobile phones

When your contract comes up for renewal, don't just renew it without thinking: there may be a contract that is cheaper for you. Try to resist the urge to get the latest phone as soon as it comes out: your life will not end if you don't have it!

Go to the SORTED! website at www.sortedfinancially.co.uk for up to date information and to download your free guide to current tax data.

88

Think about everything that you spend

If the purchase is non-essential and doesn't move you towards your goal, then don't make it!

ACTION: Make a note of any areas where you believe you can increase net income or reduce expenditure, highlight these in your income and expenditure analysis and incorporate them into your plan for the future.

Go to the SORTED! website at www.sortedfinancially.co.uk for up to date information and to download your free guide to current tax data.

89

Creating your financial plan 10

By now, you know:

- ➤ What goals you are working towards, over what timescales
- ➤ The approximate cost of those goals allowing for inflation
- ➤ The assets that you already have that you can apply towards your goals
- ➤ Your income, after tax (you may have some ideas for increasing this)
- ➤ Your expenditure, in detail (hopefully you have some ideas for reducing this)
- ➤ How much extra you may have to spend on life assurance etc to protect yourself and your family
- ➤ Therefore, the amount available to put towards your objectives in future (allowing for increases in income and reductions in expenditure).

The next step is to get the basics of your plan together – work out your strategies. How are you going to best apply the additional funds available to each of your goals? You will need to do some arithmetic or use a spreadsheet but it won't be too difficult. Your particular situation and your own priorities will

Go to the SORTED! website at www.sortedfinancially.co.uk for up to date information and to download your free guide to current tax data.

dictate what the strategies should be, but the same process applies for all.

Plan to :

1. reduce short term debt and establish an emergency fund (preferably at the same time but, if you cannot manage that, then reduce short term debt first)

2. separately, or preferably simultaneously:

   - ➤ fund for short term goals (less than five years)
   - ➤ fund for medium term goals, (five to ten years)
   - ➤ fund for long term goals (10+ years)

Short term debt

It may be that eliminating your short term debt (overdraft, credit cards and personal loans) is your goal, in itself. Maybe you find it's hard to look beyond that situation because the debt is your main anxiety – that's fine and in some ways a good thing because you will really be able to focus on getting rid of the debt. Once the debt is cleared you can look again at your other goals. However, do try to start building up an emergency cash fund at the same time as reducing the debt.

Emergency fund

The emergency fund is really important: should things go wrong, it could carry you through at least three and preferably six months' expenditure. Building up this reserve can be a big

Go to the SORTED! website at www.sortedfinancially.co.uk for up to date information and to download your free guide to current tax data.

92

challenge in itself but if you're able to achieve this you will have a really solid base on which to build your future. The existence of an emergency fund means that you are far less likely to have to borrow expensively. Don't think of it as getting in the way of your goals or slowing you up: just do it!

Save the money on cash deposit in an ISA or in a high interest, instant access account. Do not use an account which requires notice to withdraw funds. You can find up to date information about the different accounts available on lots of websites: generally you will find that online accounts offer the best interest rates.

Short, medium and long term goals

Examples of short term objectives might be to get together sufficient money to buy a car in two years, a medium term objective might be to move to a larger family home in, say, seven years and a long term objective might be planning for your retirement.

Short

Use 'cash' for saving for your short term goals. Use the best high interest account you can find or cash in an ISA if you are not using your annual ISA allowance elsewhere.

Medium

For medium term objectives, provided that you are happy to take some investment risk, use unit trusts or OEICs (preferably in an ISA if you are not using your annual ISA allowance

Go to the SORTED! website at www.sortedfinancially.co.uk for up to date information and to download your free guide to current tax data.

93

elsewhere). If you are not an experienced investor or taking any professional advice, select a 'Balanced Managed' fund initially. See section on saving and investing for more information.

Long

For long term objectives, use unit trusts or OEICs (again, preferably in an ISA if you are not using your annual ISA allowance elsewhere). Consider using a 'Growth Managed' fund initially, if you are selecting for yourself. For more information, see the section on saving and investing.

ISAs are ideal for providing for medium to long term objectives although pension plans may also be more appropriate for the latter.

How to work out strategies

➢ You know what you have to play with – the available assets.

These will be liquid, realisable assets which, unless you are planning to sell something like a car, are likely to be existing savings and investments.

➢ You know how much of your surplus disposable income you can afford to apply to achieving your goals.

➢ For each of your goals, you have calculated an estimate of the cost, making allowance for inflation.

➢ You have prioritised your goals.

Go to the SORTED! website at www.sortedfinancially.co.uk for up to date information and to download your free guide to current tax data.

94

The easiest way to deal with this is to plan to satisfy each goal, as you have prioritised them. You may wish to fund for more than one goal simultaneously, particularly for medium and long term goals: this adds some complication to the process but you can manage it, do your sums appropriately.

Take each goal, in priority order, one by one:

Will your available assets meet the cost of this goal?

> ➢ If so, how much of your available assets will remain?

> ➢ If not, how much of your disposable income would you need to apply to this goal in order to achieve it in the timescale? Use a calculator to work out how much a monthly savings amount could produce allowing for the effect of compound interest. For help, look for directions to calculators on the SORTED! website.

How much surplus disposable income, if any, is left after you have allocated what you need for the previous goal?

If you still have available assets or surplus disposable income left after allocating resources to the first goal, then move on to the second and repeat the process. Keep doing this until you run out of resources or goals. (If you run out of goals before you run out of resources then you are in exceptionally good shape.)

Go to the SORTED! website at www.sortedfinancially.co.uk for up to date information and to download your free guide to current tax data.

95

ACTION: Write down the results of the process above. This forms the basis of your plan. You know how you are allocating your available assets and the amount you can afford to save going forward towards each of your goals. From this you will be able to work out what sort of savings or investment vehicle is most appropriate for the purpose. See the section on saving and investment.

Progress

Once your have this sorted out, you will be well on your way through the process of financial planning.

> Confirm goals and objectives ✓

> Establish Net Worth statement ✓

> Analyse income and expenditure ✓

> Create strategies / plan ✓

> Implement the plan

> Regularly review

See sections on making the best of what you've got, borrowing and saving and investment for more information that you will need to consider.

Go to the SORTED! website at www.sortedfinancially.co.uk for up to date information and to download your free guide to current tax data.

96

Making the best of what you have 11

If you have some cash on deposit or investments, it is important to check that they are doing as well as they possibly can for you.

Is the asset held in the right type of account?

➢ Cash deposit – for emergency fund and short term goals

➢ Collective investments – for money that will not be required for five years or more

Is the asset getting the best possible return?

➢ Is your deposit account earning the best rate of interest available? Very often internet based accounts offer the best rates. There are lots of websites where you can compare rates available.

➢ The evaluation of longer term investment performance is more difficult: you may be able to do some research on the internet to get a view of the expectation for your investment, whatever it is, but it may be that, depending on your circumstances, you may have to get professional help. See section on saving and investing.

Go to the SORTED! website at www.sortedfinancially.co.uk for up to date information and to download your free guide to current tax data.

97

Is the asset held in the right person's name?

> ➢ If one of a couple is a non-taxpayer or a basic rate taxpayer and the other is perhaps a higher rate taxpayer, then the net return on the investment will be greater if it is in the hands of the person paying the lowest rate of tax.

Are you paying the lowest rate of interest possible on credit card and personal loan debt?

> ➢ It might be possible to transfer credit card balances to another card with nil interest for a while. See section on borrowing.

Is every advantage being taken of all tax saving opportunities?

Tax is unwelcome at the best of times but paying tax when it is unnecessary, is madness.

> ➢ Check that every advantage is being made of ISA (Individual Savings Account) allowances and, if appropriate to you, tax free products like National Savings certificates

> ➢ For most of us contributions to pension schemes are highly tax efficient for the longer term objective of retirement planning. See section on retirement planning.

Go to the SORTED! website at www.sortedfinancially.co.uk for up to date information and to download your free guide to current tax data.

98

> ➢ If you have investments outside ISAs or pensions, is use being made, on a regular basis, of the annual capital gains tax allowance?

ACTION: record any changes that you plan to make, carefully.

Go to the SORTED! website at www.sortedfinancially.co.uk for up to date information and to download your free guide to current tax data.

99

Borrowing
Credit and debt

12

Even today, it is all too easy to borrow – we are bombarded by invitations from organisations that want to lend us money. However, just because someone will lend you money doesn't mean that it's a good idea to borrow it!

Borrowings have to be repaid, usually on a strict schedule of payments, and you have to pay interest on the amount that you borrow so that in the end, you will have to find an awful lot more to repay the loan than you were able to borrow in the first place.

So, if you don't *need* to borrow – don't!

When you are tempted to borrow, think very carefully about how you will afford the repayments – what will you have to give up in order to make those payments? Crucially, relate this back to your goals – will taking the loan move you closer to where you want to be?

If it's feasible, it is better to be your own banker – it generally means waiting before you can buy something but the waiting period will not be as long as the time you would have to spend paying back a loan. If you are able to save for something over a period of time, you will be the one that earns the interest on your savings. But if you borrow to buy something now, the lender will enjoy the interest and you will have the commitment to make the repayments.

Go to the SORTED! website at www.sortedfinancially.co.uk for up to date information and to download your free guide to current tax data.

If you do need to borrow, you will find some useful loan calculators online which will help you get an idea what the monthly costs of borrowing might be and how much interest you will end up paying if you do borrow. See the SORTED! website for information.

Credit

Credit can be very useful, if used properly. Your credit card allows you to make purchases on the understanding that you will pay the credit card company back later. If you settle your credit card bill in full every month, there would not normally be any charge or interest payable.

However, credit cards are a very expensive way to borrow if you do not pay off the balance each month, or if you use them to draw cash. By all means have a credit card but make sure that you are not overspending and clear the balance every month – this way you have a fantastic facility which makes paying for things – and indeed keeping track of your spending (by analysing the statements) – simple, easy and convenient.

It is one of the great ironies of life that you need to have borrowed money in order to be allowed to borrow more. If you are applying for a mortgage, it will be very helpful to have a credit card record, provided it is a good record. So always try and repay the whole amount that you spend each month. And if you need to spread, for instance the cost of a holiday, do so carefully and in a planned way over, say, three months, and make sensible payments, well in excess of the minimum required, every month and ON TIME. This will help you avoid

Go to the SORTED! website at www.sortedfinancially.co.uk for up to date information and to download your free guide to current tax data.

102

a bad credit record which might impair your chances of borrowing what you need to buy a property, or any other major item, in the future.

When shopping online, increasingly there are quite high charges for using credit cards: you can usually use a debit card without charge so, if you can save the cost by paying directly from your current account then do.

Debt

Debt is debilitating, both practically and emotionally. Long term mortgage debt is something that many of us have to reconcile ourselves to and sometimes we may need to borrow a large sum, for instance to start a business. However, the eradication of other debts – credit card, personal loan, car purchase schemes etc – should be very high on the agenda.

Repaying debt, even though it may take some time, is liberating and frees up the monthly repayments so that we can apply those funds to something that is important to us. With credit card debt, interest is often heaped upon interest and the amount of the debt rises each month.

If you have a lot of short term debt, it is likely that at least one of your main goals will be to get yourself out of this situation. Always aim to repay the most expensive debt first. Consolidation of various debts to a single, reasonably priced, loan is well worth considering but do make sure that you will be able, consistently, to meet the required monthly payments on the consolidated debt.

Go to the SORTED! website at www.sortedfinancially.co.uk for up to date information and to download your free guide to current tax data.

Consolidating debt to reduce costs

If you have a number of expensive borrowings, this may be a time when it is advantageous to borrow – for instance, to consolidate unmanageable and expensive credit card debt or other short term loans into one arrangement to be repaid over a longer term and with lower, affordable, monthly payments.

You may find that you could get another credit card to transfer your balances to, which will give you an interest free period during which you could make real efforts to get rid of that debt. Make absolutely sure that you understand the terms and conditions: very often there is a catch. Have a look at some of the money websites to get an understanding of what is available, but remember that, depending on your credit rating, you may not be successful in your application for new credit cards.

The ultimate consolidation is to re-mortgage and to add the short term debts to the long term debt secured on your home. This is a cheaper option because the term of repayment is typically very long and because the rate of interest will typically be much lower than that payable on a credit card or short term personal loan. The downside is that it will take longer and cost more to repay the debt on your home. Also, for some it may not be possible, especially in times of tight credit, to borrow the additional funds needed on your mortgage, whereas a personal loan may be available.

Go to the SORTED! website at www.sortedfinancially.co.uk for up to date information and to download your free guide to current tax data.

104

Mortgages

Mortgages are most people's largest debt. These are sometimes arranged on a 'repayment' capital and interest repayment basis, where the monthly payments are calculated not only to pay the required interest but also to gradually repay the borrowing itself over the period of the mortgage. Mortgage interest rates may be low from an historical perspective but the monthly repayments can still be very substantial because of the need to repay capital as well as interest.

A 'repayment' mortgage is generally the best and most sensible type of mortgage to have but it may sometimes be advantageous to consider an interest only loan. Monthly payments for an interest only mortgage are much lower because each month you pay only interest to the lender and you must find another way of repaying the mortgage by the end of the mortgage term.

Interest only mortgages are not advisable for most of us for the long term but there may be occasions for the shorter term where they may be helpful: if you are borrowing for a short term project and you are expecting to receive a capital lump sum (eg from sale of another property or from inheritance) or, as a short term measure, if you are trying to minimise costs in order concentrate on repaying other, more expensive, debt (eg credit card debt).

If you are unsure about the terms of your mortgage, ask your lender to explain or consult an independent mortgage adviser.

Go to the SORTED! website at www.sortedfinancially.co.uk for up to date information and to download your free guide to current tax data.

105

Problems with debt

If you have problems with debt, don't panic! There are things that you can do to improve the situation: the important thing is to face up to the problem and start doing something about it NOW. Don't wait another week. By taking action immediately, you will at least stop the situation getting worse.

You have the tools you need: you have already done most of the preparatory work to allow you to crack the situation. Go back to your Net Worth statement where you have listed out all the debts. Decide which is the most important /urgent and focus on this first.

Work out the total that, allowing for any other savings on expenditure that you can make, would be the maximum that you could afford to use as repayments each month. Allocate these repayments across your various debts and see what, if any, shortfalls there are. If there are shortfalls, contact the lenders, in writing, and let them have a copy of your monthly budget. Explain that you are anxious to resolve the situation as quickly as you can and offer to pay a monthly amount that you know you can afford.

Bear in mind that each lender will naturally want to get the most they can out of your total budget for monthly repayments. If they agree to the arrangement, make sure that you make the promised payments on time!

If you feel that a lender is putting unacceptable pressure on you, refer them to the Office of Fair Trading who regulate the provision of consumer credit.

Go to the SORTED! website at www.sortedfinancially.co.uk for up to date information and to download your free guide to current tax data.

Getting help if you are in trouble

If, after looking at all your options for repayment, you feel you can't resolve the situation on your own, there is help and advice available.

If you are in real trouble with your debt get help from the Citizens Advice Bureau or National Debtline (search online). There are many other organisations that can help you, free of charge – such as the Consumer Credit Counselling Service or Payplan. Armed with your budget and net worth statement, they will be able to help you to formulate a plan. They can also help with what to say and do when dealing with your existing creditors. Some organisations may even help you prepare for a court hearing, if things have got to that stage.

There are debt management companies that will help you sort out a repayment schedule etc, for a fee. These may be useful as a last resort but if you can get the help and advice that you need free of charge, why pay for it?

Credit Rating

Bear in mind that, if you have been failing to make due payments on the existing debts, you will not have a good credit record and therefore a poor credit rating, so it may be difficult to borrow or you may be charged a penal rate of interest.

If you have problems with a bad credit history and you are on the way to sorting out your problems, you can get help to repair

Go to the SORTED! website at www.sortedfinancially.co.uk for up to date information and to download your free guide to current tax data.

107

your credit history, free of charge, at UK Credit Repair (search online).

Student Loans

Increased student tuition fees have brought student debt right to the top of the list of considerations for young people. Some young people will decide not to go to university and perhaps get an apprenticeship instead, others will leave university with very large amounts of debt: do your best not to be one of the latter.

If you are studying for 3 or 4 years, you will need to think very seriously about getting a part time job while you are studying and certainly getting jobs in the vacations. Very few parents will be in a position to meet all of the costs of university education for you, even supposing they were prepared to, and you would be foolish to start off your working life saddled with huge debts if you can help it.

Student loans are normally available to cover the cost of tuition at university and may also be available for maintenance costs for full time students whose families have low incomes.

Whereas student loans used to represent a cheap means of borrowing, this is no longer the case (for loans from 2012 at least) and interest at above inflation is typically added.

Generally speaking you do not have to start repaying student loans until your earnings are above a certain threshold: check the SORTED! website for up to date limits. This may give you

Go to the SORTED! website at www.sortedfinancially.co.uk for up to date information and to download your free guide to current tax data.

108

the chance to build up an emergency fund before the loan repayments compulsorily kick in: if so, do take that opportunity - it will be harder once your student loan payments begin.

Student loans do not generally affect your ability to borrow and they do not affect your credit rating but, if you are applying for a personal loan or mortgage which is calculated on your ability to meet monthly repayments, your student loan payments will be taken into account.

Since repayments are compulsory once you are earning above the threshold, you will need to factor this in when prioritising other loan repayments.

For more detail about student loans, including the regime that existed before 2012, go to www.direct.go.uk and search for student loans.

ACTION: make a list of anything you plan to do and any further research you plan to do.

Go to the SORTED! website at www.sortedfinancially.co.uk for up to date information and to download your free guide to current tax data.

109

Saving and Investing

13

Saving

Saving is the process of accumulating funds, generally from income, which can either be used to reduce debt, to provide an 'emergency' fund or to fund specific or general goals.

Suitable vehicles

As a start, a bank or building society or National Savings deposit account will do – the important thing is to start!

You will find it very helpful to have an account for savings which is separate from your day to day current account so that you can see the money accumulating and it doesn't 'disappear' into other funds.

Set up a standing order from your current account to your savings account about a week after your salary or other regular income is due to go in, for your basic saving (the amount that you know you can afford to save each month). If you find that you have spare cash at other times, make a transfer of an appropriate amount on a one-off basis.

Individual Savings Accounts (ISAs)

These are tax wrapper accounts within which you can hold a range of different investments. The big advantage of ISAs is that you pay no tax on income or capital gains: with generous

Go to the SORTED! website at www.sortedfinancially.co.uk for up to date information and to download your free guide to current tax data.

111

annual allowances for ISA saving, this means that you could accumulate very large sums over a number of years which you can access at any time without having to consider any tax consequence. Within the ISA itself, investments suffer no tax on interest or dividends (other than dividends from UK companies) or on capital gains realised which means that the value should increase more quickly than an equivalent cash deposit or investment held outside an ISA.

See the SORTED! website for information about the limits on ISAs etc.

You should remember that it is a case of 'use it or lose it' with ISA allowances – if you don't use your allowance before the end of the tax year, you will not be able to get it back in future and will have missed the opportunity to get that money into the tax free world.

There are two types of ISA investment: cash and stocks & shares. You can open no more than one cash ISA and one stocks & shares ISA each tax year.

The rule is that no more than half of the annual allowance can be invested in a cash ISA but there is no similar restriction for stocks & shares ISAs. You don't have to put any money in a cash ISA: instead the full allowance can be invested in a stocks & shares account if that is more appropriate, which it may well be.

Various non-cash assets can be held within a stocks & shares ISA. These most normally include unit trusts, open ended

Go to the SORTED! website at www.sortedfinancially.co.uk for up to date information and to download your free guide to current tax data.

112

investment companies, shares and investment trusts. Savers and investors who initially invested in cash in an ISA can transfer that money into a stocks & shares account without losing the tax free status. However, you cannot move the other way, ie from stocks & shares to cash.

If possible, you should make full use of your ISA allowance, particularly for the medium to long term objectives because maximum advantage can be gained from the tax advantages of ISAs in the longer term.

Children

Think about instilling some old-fashioned principles of saving in your kids, from an early age. There are lots of basic savings accounts available for children, from National Savings, banks or building societies. Getting into the habit of putting away a bit of their pocket money each week, or the 'tenner' from Auntie Mary, towards a sensible goal will give them great satisfaction and the habit will stand them in good stead for the future.

Children enjoy full personal allowance for income tax and annual allowance for capital gains tax: their savings should be tax free in most cases.

Junior ISAs

The introduction of Junior ISAs means that, from birth, it is possible to save in a tax efficient way for your children's further education or for their first car and driving lessons or the cost of setting up their first independent home, or simply to

Go to the SORTED! website at www.sortedfinancially.co.uk for up to date information and to download your free guide to current tax data.

113

accumulate a sum which can switch directly into a full ISA when the child reaches 18 to give them a flying start in terms of tax free saving for their future. The Junior ISA is the property of the child and nothing can be taken out of it until they are 18.

In the same way as adult ISAs, there are two types – cash and stocks & shares: the two types of account can be used as alternatives or in combination. If it will be some years before the child reaches 18 then a stocks & shares account will probably be most sensible initially. (see Investing section)

Parents and grandparents (or indeed anybody else) can add relatively modest amounts to the Junior ISA each year (see the SORTED! website for details) which may make a lot more sense than heaping more and more toys or gadgets or expensive clothes (which they may not need or even really want) on the child. This could amount to a sizeable nest egg over the years and your child will be very glad of it.

The perceived 'problem' with Junior ISAs is that, at age 18, your child will obtain full access to the funds that have been saved: the trick therefore is to educate them to apply them wisely or even not to spend them if they are not really required. This will test the values that you've instilled in your child!

Child Trust Funds

These tax free savings vehicles, which were available for children born between September 2002 and the beginning of January 2011, are substantially the same as Junior ISAs. There are some differences and CTFs are slightly less flexible than Junior ISAs but the same limits for investment each year and

Go to the SORTED! website at www.sortedfinancially.co.uk for up to date information and to download your free guide to current tax data.

114

the same rules about funds not being available until age 18 apply. The Government used to make contributions to CTFs at birth and at age 7 but, in most cases, that no longer applies.

Those children who have a Child Trust Fund will not be able to have a Junior ISA as well but will be able to maintain the Child Trust Fund.

More information is available from www.direct.gov.uk: search for Child Trust Funds.

Investing

Investing is for the longer term – you need to be willing to tie up your money and take some risk, in order to get a better return than that available from cash. It may mean having a short term loss in order to have the opportunity to make a long-term gain.

You can invest lump sums of capital or regular monthly amounts, from as little as £50 per month.

Risk

The theory of investment is that greater potential returns are the reward for risk in the long term. Note the greater reward is *potential* and not guaranteed and that you need to be taking a long term view with riskier investments.

No investment is completely risk-free. You need to decide how comfortable you are with the prospect of the value of your

Go to the SORTED! website at www.sortedfinancially.co.uk for up to date information and to download your free guide to current tax data.

115

investment dropping either in the short term before values recover or, in the worst case, permanently.

Tolerance of risk is different for each of us and varies according to our personality, our circumstances and the term for which we are planning to invest.

> ➤ If you are likely to lie awake at night worrying about the value of your assets then you should avoid high risk investments that tend to be more volatile in value than less risky investments.

> ➤ If you have very little money, don't gamble it on high risk investments because you cannot afford to lose it.

> ➤ If you plan to spend that money in the relatively short term you cannot afford the risk that the value might fall and so high risk investments are not suitable for the purpose.

Remember that even though the value of your investment may go down, this is only a 'paper' loss and you will only make an actual loss (or indeed gain) if you sell your investment.

It is assumed in what follows that you are not particularly risk averse.

Asset Classes

Asset classes describe different types of investments that have different characteristics and therefore different applications.

Go to the SORTED! website at www.sortedfinancially.co.uk for up to date information and to download your free guide to current tax data.

116

The four main asset classes are:

➢ Cash
➢ Bonds
➢ Property
➢ Shares (equities)

Cash is money deposited with an institution in return for an agreed rate of interest.

Bonds are issued, either by government (these are called Gilts in the UK) or a corporation, when you lend them money at an agreed fixed rate of interest (payable each year) over a predetermined period. Your original investment is usually returned to you at redemption on a specified date in the future. Bonds can be bought and sold at any time but the sale or purchase price will not be the same as the ultimate redemption value: the value of bonds tends to fluctuate according to general economic conditions, the strength of the organisation to which the money has been lent and prevailing interest rates at the time.

Property is generally, in investment terms, commercial property and not residential property *. Commercial property includes shops, offices, warehouses etc. Investors expect to receive rental income and to be able to sell the asset again in future, hopefully at a profit. This asset class can be complicated by the fact that it is not always possible to find a buyer, on demand, for a large commercial building and therefore it may not be possible to sell the asset when required. Capital values of commercial property vary according to the general economic conditions, the demand for that type of property and demand

Go to the SORTED! website at www.sortedfinancially.co.uk for up to date information and to download your free guide to current tax data.

117

in the area where it is located. The value is also dependent on the quality of tenant to which the property is let (interpreted as the likelihood that their business will be sufficiently successful to enable the tenant to continue to pay the rent for the term of the lease).

Shares are purchased when you buy a stake in a particular company. Investors in shares hope to receive dividend income or capital growth in the value of the share or a combination of the two. Shares are traded on stock markets and prices vary according to general economic conditions, the strength of the corporation, the demand for investment in the corporation's sector and market sentiment. Prices can fluctuate widely – this is known as volatility.

* *Residential property.* Some people invest in residential property – buy to let – but this is a rather different thing and, although there is appeal in owning bricks and mortar, it is higher risk than you might think. Buy to let investors typically have most of their eggs in the residential property market (hence their investments are not diversified), and may have only one buy to let property: they are responsible for the costs of maintenance of the property and are vulnerable to rises in interest rates and falls in property values because most borrow heavily against the property. In addition, they are vulnerable to periods of time when the property is not let, to getting 'bad' tenants who do not pay their rent or 'trash the place' and who are very difficult to get rid of. Rental receipts, after expenses and any capital gain made on the sale of the property, are both subject to tax. Buy to let can work out extremely well but there are many occasions when it doesn't so be aware of the risks.

Go to the SORTED! website at www.sortedfinancially.co.uk for up to date information and to download your free guide to current tax data.

Some people regard their own home as an investment, taking advantage of their ability to borrow in their younger days to invest in a house which they hope will increase in value over the years and allow them to sell and downsize when they retire or when their children leave home, releasing a capital sum. This can be very attractive particularly since, under the present regime, any capital gain that you make on your 'principal residence' when you sell it is tax free, but there can be drawbacks for some:

➤ The existence of a large debt may cause one or another of the parties involved anxiety, particularly if the interest rate payable may rise or if employment is not secure.

➤ The values of houses may fall as well as rise.

➤ The cost of moving from one house to another is high and the higher the value of the house the higher the associated costs: moving to another area may be unavoidable.

Diversification

Whatever the size of your investment portfolio, and whether or not you are experienced at investment, your portfolio (the investments in total) should be as diversified as possible between asset classes. Overall this will reduce risk as, providing the asset classes are not too closely related (correlated), there is a good chance that when one part of your portfolio is doing badly, another will be doing well to prop up the value of the portfolio overall. This is the most effective way to reduce risk in investing.

Go to the SORTED! website at www.sortedfinancially.co.uk for up to date information and to download your free guide to current tax data.

119

Pooled investments

Unless you are an experienced investor or are getting advice from an expert, it is best to use pooled, or collective, investments. This type of investment includes unit trusts, OEICs, Exchange Traded Funds and investment trusts as well as pension funds. Lots of people's money is pooled into a fund to buy stocks and shares, fixed interest investments, property and so on, the actual mix of investments, the asset classes involved and sometimes the geographic region in which they may invest depending on the remit of the manager of the fund. Typically, in return for a fee, the investment manager decides on the holdings that make up the fund and on the timing of buying or selling the holdings in the fund.

Active v passive investment

A continuing debate rages about whether the management that active fund managers bring in researching closely which shares etc to buy in their funds, actually pays off in the end given that there is considerable cost involved in the process and, inevitably, they do not always get it right. The passive supporters camp says that the important thing is to choose the correct asset classes in the correct proportions and then simply buy passive or 'index tracker' funds to provide the exposure to each asset class required.

Passive investment is gaining in popularity and has considerably lower costs than actively managed funds.

If you are not confident, it is simplest to select a managed fund where the manager is going to make the call on asset allocation

Go to the SORTED! website at www.sortedfinancially.co.uk for up to date information and to download your free guide to current tax data.

120

and then either buy passive investment instruments to construct the portfolio within the fund or else to actively manage both the asset allocation and the stock selection decisions. Try to find funds where the charges are not too high: you will find that these are lower in 'passive' than 'active' funds.

If you are interested in constructing your own passive investment portfolio, there is advice available online and you can buy the passive funds needed, online, very cheaply.

Ethical Investment

Some people feel strongly that they do not wish their investments to support companies that do not have ethical or socially responsible policies – for instance those that may deal in armaments or tobacco. A wide range of funds (SRI funds) exist which are suitable for investors who prefer to restrict their investment in this way. This is a specialist area – you can find a number of websites that can help you (see the SORTED! website) if you are serious about this but do try to remember that you should still be looking for a good spread of asset classes and geographic regions within your portfolio of investments.

Investment period

For short term objectives, we need to be able to rely on the value of the investment, which makes cash an attractive asset class. We know that there is no possibility of losing a cash investment unless the bank or other institution to whom you 'lend' your money goes bust in which case there would almost

Go to the SORTED! website at www.sortedfinancially.co.uk for up to date information and to download your free guide to current tax data.

121

certainly be some compensation payable. There has been some anxiety about this recently for the first time for many, many years – so remember, at the time of writing, up to £85,000 of money on deposit with any one banking institution is 100% protected by legislation. The only other risk associated with cash is that, in the longer term, inflation reduces the real value of the money: this is why cash is generally not an asset class recommended for long term investment (other than in your emergency fund).

As a general rule, do not invest in unit trusts, OEICS or other collective investments that are linked to stock markets or bond markets, or in direct share holdings in companies, unless your plan allows you to leave those funds invested for five years or more.

Use cash for the short-term. In the longer term, the other asset classes should provide a superior return as compared to cash deposits. However, this potential out-performance comes at the expense of risk, which we can best explain as volatility in value, in the interim. As a general rule the longer the term of the investment the less the risk that, at the time that you need access to those funds, prices will have fallen below that at which you originally purchased. Ideally you would be in a position such that you did not *need* to sell this type of investment if, at the appointed time, the values were badly depressed. If possible you would wait for things to improve.

For medium term objectives (five to ten years), use collective investment vehicles, perhaps within an ISA, and, if you are not an experienced investor or taking any professional advice,

Go to the SORTED! website at www.sortedfinancially.co.uk for up to date information and to download your free guide to current tax data.

122

select a 'Balanced Managed' fund which will provide a spread of different asset classes and investment types appropriate for the medium term. Once within three years of your target date, switch funds to 'Cautious Managed' and ultimately to cash at least a year before your target date or wait until nearer the target date (at least 2 years) and switch directly to cash from the Balanced fund.

For long term objectives (more than 10 years), use collective investments perhaps within an ISA or pension plan. Consider using a 'Growth Managed' fund if you are selecting for yourself. Once within 7 years of the target date, move your investments to 'Balanced Managed' funds, then to 'Cautious Managed' funds and cash (see above).

Capital Gains Tax

If you are investing outside ISAs or pension funds, try to make best use of the annual exemption for capital gains tax. Take profits where they are available by selling some of the investments that are showing a profit. It is always difficult to know how much to sell but, as a tip for the inexperienced, if you have a fund that has done well, consider selling sufficient to reduce your holding to the original amount that you committed to that particular fund.

Common pitfalls of investing

The psychology of investing reveals some interesting theories about why people tend to act illogically regarding their investments and therefore are not successful. Here are just a

Go to the SORTED! website at www.sortedfinancially.co.uk for up to date information and to download your free guide to current tax data.

123

few general rules that it is helpful to follow and pitfalls which should be avoided.

Fear of loss

We all have the tendency to make the same mistakes when investing: it is very hard to make rational decisions, particularly about selling investments. We hate to lose, more than we like to win. Because of this we tend to avoid action that may lead to regret and so avoid feeling regret. This may lead to holding on to poor investments too long or selling good ones too early. Try to be methodical about it, be realistic and don't be greedy.

Timing markets

It is impossible to effectively 'time' markets, ie. know when the market is at the bottom or when it is at the top. A very common tendency of individual investors is to buy something when they have heard consistent reports of rising prices, ie when they feel buoyed up by the reports that they have heard and feel confident to buy. They will then typically hold the investment until the price has been falling for some time and they lose confidence in the stock and sell. What has been achieved is a purchase at a high price and sale at a low price – disaster. So try to stick with your investment unless you have some reason to be concerned that it is under-performing, in which case replace it with a similar investment but stay invested until the time comes when you need access to the money or need to reduce the risk exposure as the target date approaches.

Go to the SORTED! website at www.sortedfinancially.co.uk for up to date information and to download your free guide to current tax data.

124

Pound-cost-averaging

This weird expression describes the process of investing or dis-investing gradually over a period of time. If you are unsure if this is the right time to cash in an investment (*might the market go up, or indeed down, the day after you cash in?*) then adopt a gradual approach and sell the holding in several tranches, perhaps monthly over a period of a few months. The same technique can be applied when buying, and reduces the risk of committing to one big purchase or sale on one day, at one price.

Inheritance

When we have inherited something from a parent or respected relative, there is a lack of rational decision making about selling. This is most commonly seen with shares in 'traditional' UK companies. "If my father thought they were a good investment then they must be ...." Well, they may well have been when your father bought them: that doesn't mean they are a good investment now nor that these shares are appropriate to your present circumstances. They may be too high risk and they may represent too high a percentage of your total investments. Try to be dispassionate about investments.

Tips from 'the man down at the pub'

It is possible that this chap is a professional investment expert although if he were, is he likely to spend his Friday nights in the pub talking about his work? More likely he is anything but professional or expert and just because he has convinced himself that he has been clever with an investment does not mean that he will be right in the long term nor that this

Go to the SORTED! website at www.sortedfinancially.co.uk for up to date information and to download your free guide to current tax data.

125

investment is appropriate to your needs at this time. It's best to avoid taking his advice.

Getting help

There are a number of websites available that give information and suggestions for investment, although this can sometimes be complicated. Go to the SORTED! website for suggested online resources.

If you feel out of your depth seek advice from a financial planner or an independent financial adviser.

ACTION: make a written plan for what arrangements you would like to put in place as a result of considering this chapter.

Go to the SORTED! website at www.sortedfinancially.co.uk for up to date information and to download your free guide to current tax data.

126

Implementing your plan
Making it happen

14

Have a good look at your list of strategies as well as the list of other things that need to be done. There is a lot to do to implement your plans – you just need to start!

You may need to do any one or all of the following and possibly more besides:

➢ Arrange to have a will drawn up

➢ Arrange life assurance or other protection policies

➢ Start a pension plan or join your employer's scheme

➢ Put your new controlled expenditure regime into force

➢ Maybe apply for a new or additional job

➢ Sort out the loft and do a car boot sale

➢ Check all your existing savings and investments are in the best place

➢ Open new savings or investment accounts, as dictated by your plan

➢ Set up standing orders for saving

➢ Rearrange your credit card borrowing

➢ Consolidate debts

There is only one way to tackle it: just do it - as efficiently as you can.

Go to the SORTED! website at www.sortedfinancially.co.uk for up to date information and to download your free guide to current tax data.

127

Progress

- ➢ Confirm goals and objectives ✓

- ➢ Establish Net Worth statement ✓

- ➢ Analyse income and expenditure ✓

- ➢ Create strategies / plan ✓

- ➢ Implement the plan ✓

- ➢ Regularly review

Go to the SORTED! website at www.sortedfinancially.co.uk for up to date information and to download your free guide to current tax data.

128

Reviewing your plan

15

It is vital to review your plan regularly. Remember that all the estimates you have made for the cost of achieving your goals, the value of your invested assets in the future, your income and expenditure in the future has been just that – estimates. By reviewing everything on a regular basis, these estimates are kept closer to reality.

The appropriate frequency will depend on the timescale for your goals. If you are working really hard to repay all your short term debt within one year then you should check your progress and the strategies you are employing every couple of months. If you are working towards a retirement goal, a long time in the future, then once a year is probably sufficient to check how you are doing. Either way, keep on top of it.

Do it all over again
Whatever your circumstances, you should do a full review at least once a year.

Go right back to the beginning of the book and start by rescoring your Life Circle – are the scores better?

Go to the SORTED! website at www.sortedfinancially.co.uk for up to date information and to download your free guide to current tax data.

129

1. Review your goals – perhaps you have some new ones or the existing ones have changed slightly. You will need to re-calculate the estimated cost of each of your goals.

2. Re-calculate your assets and liabilities and therefore your net worth – this will hopefully have improved since the last time.

3. Re-do your income and expenditure analysis. What is your net income surplus (or deficit)? Does this show an improvement on last time?

4. Check that the protection you have in place for yourself and your family is still appropriate. If you have changed jobs, different employee benefits may now apply or there may have been other changes in your life – perhaps the arrival of a child.

5. The budget that you put in place last time needs review. Have you been able to stick to your planned expenditure? Are you able to make any further improvement?

6. Create a new plan with new strategies appropriate to your situation now.

7. Put these strategies into force!

8. Come back to review again, in future.

Go to the SORTED! website at www.sortedfinancially.co.uk for up to date information and to download your free guide to current tax data.

Spare pages have been provided at the back of this book to allow you to record your review process.

You will also need to evaluate the performance and appropriateness of your savings and investment vehicles each time you review your situation.

> ➤ Are you still getting the best available interest rates on your deposit accounts?

> ➤ Have you and your partner made best use of your ISA allowance(s)?

> ➤ Are your longer term investments performing OK relative to other similar ones available? (Don't make changes for change's sake).

> ➤ Is the asset allocation (the investment mix) of your longer term investments still about right?

> ➤ If you are now within 7 years of the date when you plan to use that money to achieve your goal, is the risk that you are taking with the investment still appropriate?

> ➤ If you are within 3 years of your target date, should you move some to cash deposit?

Go to the SORTED! website at www.sortedfinancially.co.uk for up to date information and to download your free guide to current tax data.

131

Progress

> ➤ Confirm goals and objectives ✓

> ➤ Establish Net Worth statement ✓

> ➤ Analyse income and expenditure ✓

> ➤ Create strategies / plan ✓

> ➤ Implement the plan ✓

> ➤ Regularly review ✓

ACTION: make a clear dairy date for the next time when you feel it would be appropriate to do a review.

Go to the SORTED! website at www.sortedfinancially.co.uk for up to date information and to download your free guide to current tax data.

132

If at first you don't succeed, try, try again

16

If this process has not worked for you, think carefully about why not.

> ➤ Were your goals really important to you? If you were not sufficiently motivated to put in the effort and make the sacrifices, then you will not have been able to stick at it.

> ➤ Were your goals realistic considering your circumstances? Re-examine the goals and try to concentrate on something that it relatively easy to achieve so that you can feel the buzz of having done it and more able to move on to something else.

> ➤ Are you being too hard on yourselves – cutting down too much on expenditure and making life miserable? This might be connected to an unrealistic goal or an unrealistic timescale.

> ➤ Are you and your partner working together? If not, why not? You need to share the goals or there won't be motivation on both sides.

> ➤ Did you share your plans with a friend or relative who could encourage you and be supportive?

> ➤ Perhaps there has been an unfortunate change in your circumstances and you may feel that you are struggling. If so, you should acknowledge it.

Go to the SORTED! website at www.sortedfinancially.co.uk for up to date information and to download your free guide to current tax data.

Winston Churchill said *'When you are going through hell, keep going'* – sound advice. The same gentleman also said:

'Never, never, never give up'

If things have changed, you need to revise your goals and your plan accordingly. Go back to the beginning of the book and try again.

Go to the SORTED! website at www.sortedfinancially.co.uk for up to date information and to download your free guide to current tax data.

134

Enjoying the fruits of your labour 17

When you achieve your first goal, however small, it will feel *so good*. You have taken control of your situation, you have put in the work, been disciplined, made sacrifices and you have achieved what you set out to do.

Congratulations!

Go out and celebrate. Enjoy whatever it is that you have been working to achieve. You deserve it.

Take note of how this achievement makes you feel and this will inspire you to go on to your next goal – and then the next and the next.

In reality, this process of goal setting, planning and achieving may never end for some people although, over the years the nature of the goals and the plans themselves will inevitably alter.

You are SORTED!

Go to the SORTED! website at www.sortedfinancially.co.uk for up to date information and to download your free guide to current tax data.

135

Appendix 1 : Life Circle

Life Circle (version 1)

Think carefully about this. Each section represents a different aspect of your life. Circle the score which most closely reflects how happy you are with that part of your life.

5 is excellent, 1 is very poor.

Date: ....

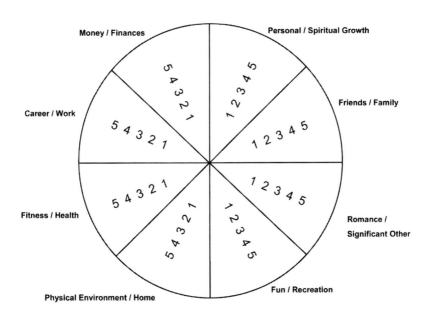

Go to the SORTED! website at www.sortedfinancially.co.uk for up to date information and to download your free guide to current tax data.

137

Life Circle (version 2)

Think carefully about this. Each section represents a different aspect of your life. Circle the score which most closely reflects how happy you are with that part of your life.

5 is excellent, 1 is very poor.

Date: ....

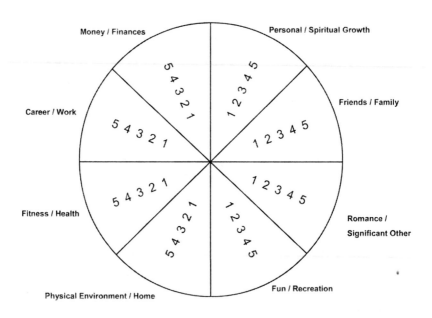

Go to the SORTED! website at www.sortedfinancially.co.uk for up to date information and to download your free guide to current tax data.

138

Life Circle (version 3)

Think carefully about this. Each section represents a different aspect of your life. Circle the score which most closely reflects how happy you are with that part of your life.

5 is excellent, 1 is very poor.

Date: ....

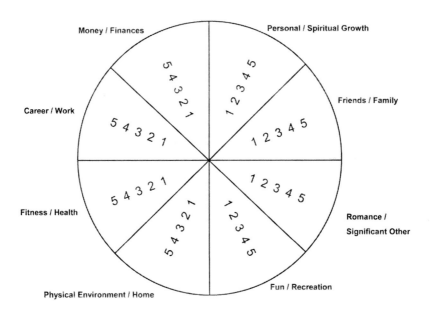

Go to the SORTED! website at www.sortedfinancially.co.uk for up to date information and to download your free guide to current tax data.

139

Appendix 2 : Goals

Goals (version 1)

Date: ....

GOAL	TIMESCALE

Go to the SORTED! website at www.sortedfinancially.co.uk for up to date information and to download your free guide to current tax data.

141

Goals (version 2)

Date: ....

GOAL	TIMESCALE

Go to the SORTED! website at www.sortedfinancially.co.uk for up to date information and to download your free guide to current tax data.

Goals (version 3)

Date: ....

GOAL	TIMESCALE

Go to the SORTED! website at www.sortedfinancially.co.uk for up to date information and to download your free guide to current tax data.

143

CPSIA information can be obtained at www.ICGtesting.com
Printed in the USA
LVOW121509010312

271191LV00010B/157/P

Appendix 3 : Net Worth Statement

Net worth statement (version 1)

Date: ....

Assets		Liabilities	
Item	Value	Item	Value
Total Assets	£	**Total Liabilities**	£

Net worth = Assets – Liabilities = £.....................

Net worth statement (version 2)

Date: ....

Assets		Liabilities	
Item	Value	Item	Value
Total Assets	£	Total Liabilities	£

Net worth = Assets – Liabilities = £.....................

Go to the SORTED! website at www.sortedfinancially.co.uk for up to date information and to download your free guide to current tax data.

Net worth statement (version 3)

Date: ……. ………………..

Assets		Liabilities	
Item	Value	Item	Value
Total Assets	£	Total Liabilities	£

Net worth = Assets – Liabilities = £…………………